THE ARMIZARE

— WORKBOOK —

Part One: The Beginner's Course

Guy Windsor

Published by Spada Press

© Guy Windsor and Spada Press 2022

ISBN 978-952-7157-86-2 The Armizare Workbook, part one: Beginner's Course RH

ISBN 978-952-7157-87-9 The Armizare Workbook, part one: Beginner's Course LH

ISBN 978-952-7157-88-6 The Armizare Workbook, part one: Beginner's Course epub

This book belongs to:

………………………………………………………………………………………..

Date begun: …………………………..

Date completed: ……………………….

TABLE OF CONTENTS

TABLE OF CONTENTS
BY MANUSCRIPT ORDER

This only includes the actions and plays that are explicitly described in the Getty or Pisani-Dossi manuscript.

ABRAZARE

DAGGER

LONGSWORD

INTRODUCTION

Welcome to the wonderful world of medieval martial arts. This workbook will show you how to begin training in Armizare, the knightly combat system of Fiore dei Liberi. I will include a significant amount of detail about Fiore's life and the book he wrote, *Il Fior di Battaglia* (The Flower of Battle) because many students are interested, but if you want to skip it for now, that's fine. The whole point of this workbook is that you, the owner, are in charge of your own training.

The problem with most training manuals (including the nine that I have written so far) is they do not take the needs of the individual reader into account. They can't – the book is a fixed linear path through the material which constrains the student to learn in the way the instructor wants to teach, or a reference work like an encyclopaedia, which would require the student to know what they wanted to look up in advance. Fine for advanced students, not much use for beginners.

But I always, always try to instil self-direction into my students. My job is to make myself redundant. I do this in practice by giving even beginners in their very first class some agency to choose what we cover. By the time they get to the seniors class (usually in a year or two), classes are entirely student led: we cover whatever they need my help with that day.

How to convey that in a workbook? Books are a very linear model, and while I can lay out my usual path through the enormous range of the Fiore syllabus, that essentially restricts agency to an unfortunate degree. But actually, very few of my readers ever read from cover to cover. Everyone skips ahead to the things they are most interested in. And why not? You've bought the book, so you can do whatever you want with it.

So I have figured out how to include gradually increasing levels of choice for the reader/ student in these workbooks. The series comprises four workbooks, each with four 'classes', presenting about as much stuff as I'd cover in a single 90-minute class. In the first class of the first book, you get one simple choice. In the second class, there's more freedom. By the time you get to the last four classes, you can choose which classes you want to take next, based on your needs and interests. At every stage, if you need prior material to successfully approach the topic at hand, that will be flagged up. So even if you skipped that class for some reason, you can go to the specific prerequisite material and practise that before returning to the thing you want to do next.

There are as many correct paths through the syllabus as there are students to walk them. In this new series I have finally figured out how to represent that on the page.

Every technique, every drill, is presented as written instructions and video clips, linked to with a QR code on the relevant page. There is abundant space for your own written notes, which is especially necessary when you are not working through the material in the order it appears in the text.

It's a choose-your-own-path training manual. You will end up covering everything, but do it as far as is practicable in the order that suits you best.

The one thing I will insist on (though obviously I'm not there so can't actually enforce it) is that you read the safety instructions first. Please. You can't train if you're broken, and you won't want to train if you've broken someone else.

In this workbook series I won't be going into the reasons behind my interpretation – the 'why I think it's done this way'. I have covered that in depth and detail in *From Medieval Manuscript to Modern Practice: The Longsword Techniques of Fiore dei Liberi* and other books.

In keeping with the 'choose your own path' idea, feel free to skip the rest of the introduction and go straight to the physical practice. I'll refer you back to various sections of the introduction as and when I think they become critical for your ability to do the techniques in question.

Regarding the videos, I've borrowed the clips from my various online courses and other resources. I'm writing this during a global pandemic, where training in person is very difficult to arrange, and I can't travel to my usual salles. This means that some of the clips are rather old. But don't worry: the links in this book are directed through my website, so as and when I can shoot better video I can redirect the link to the newer clip.

You might be wondering who I am (though honestly most of my readers buy my books because they've taken classes with me, so I nearly forgot this bit). I began working on historical fencing sources in 1993, which led to co-founding the Dawn Duellists Society in 1994, the same year that I first came across a very poor photocopy of the Pisani-Dossi manuscript. After seven years of running the Dawn Duellists Society, I moved to Helsinki, Finland, and opened the School of European Swordsmanship, teaching historical martial arts full time. From the beginning (on 17 March 2001) I've made my living researching and teaching these arts, with *Il Fior di Battaglia* as my primary source. I have many thousands of hours of research, training, and teaching under my belt, and my interpretation has been tested in the salle and in other environments such as competitive fencing, and consulting colleagues in other martial arts. I test every interpretation with blunt swords, both fast and slow, and with sharp swords both fast and slow. At every stage I have been publishing my results, and learning from the responses I get from the historical martial arts community. This began with the publication of my first book, *The Swordsman's Companion*, in 2004, and I've produced three other books on Fiore's art so far. This is in addition to translating Vadi's *De Arte Gladiatoria Dimicandi* (published as *The Art of Sword Fighting in Earnest*), writing the definitive guide to Capoferro's rapier fencing (*The Duellist's Companion*, 2006), a set of four workbooks for learning rapier fencing, and three more general works, *Swordfighting for Writers, Game Designers, and Martial Artists*, *The Theory and Practice of Historical Martial Arts*, and *The Windsor Method: The Principles of Solo Training*.

In 2013 I created the Syllabus Wiki, which put the syllabi I have created (for Fiore, Capoferro, Vadi, and other sources) online in video format for free. I travel all over the world to teach seminars, so I have seen my interpretations practised by thousands of people from dozens of countries and backgrounds.

As you can see, transparency is all: I need people to know what my interpretations are so they can comment, criticise, agree, disagree, and in general help me improve them. In the quest for similar feedback on my academic work, I submitted three of my books to Edinburgh University for a PhD by research publications, which they granted (after much travail) in 2018.

None of this means I'm right, of course. But I certainly know the sources inside out and backwards, can work with them in their original languages, can execute my interpretation at speed under pressure, and have taught hundreds, maybe thousands of others to do the same.

This workbook is based on the Beginners' Course curriculum I developed over 15 years of running my school. You tell me how well it works for you!

Safety

When training with weapons you hold your partner's life in your hands. This is a sacred trust and must not be abused.

Disclaimer: I accept no responsibility of any kind for injuries you sustain while you are not under my direct personal supervision. During this course you will be taught how to create safe training drills, and I am certain that if you follow the instructions there is a very low likelihood of injury. But if I am not there in person to create and sustain a safe training environment, I cannot be held responsible for any accidents that may occur.

The basic principles of safe training are:

1. Respect: for the art, your training partners, the weapons, and yourself.

2. Caution: assume everything is dangerous unless you have reason to believe otherwise.

3. Know your limits. Just because it's safe for somebody else, does not necessarily mean it's safe for you. Never train or fence when you are tired, angry, or in any state of mind or body that makes accidents and injuries more likely.

Most groups that keep going for more than a year have a pretty good set of safety guidelines in place. Make sure you know what they are, and follow them.

My senior students routinely train with sharp swords, often with no protection. That's not as dangerous as it sounds, when you remember that they have been training usually for five-plus years at that point, under my supervision.

You cannot afford time off training for stupid injuries. Life's too short. Whatever training you are doing must must must leave you healthier than when you started it. You will not win Olympic gold medals this way, but you won't end up breaking yourself either. The path to sporting glory is littered with the shattered bodies and minds of the unlucky many who broke themselves on the way. Don't join them.

Who was Fiore dei Liberi?

Fiore dei Liberi was a master of the art of arms (which he called *armizare*). He was born some time around 1350, and died some time after 1410. Most of what we know about his life comes from the introduction to his manuscripts, and from research done by Francesco Novati (who published the Pisani-Dossi manuscript in facsimile in 1902) and Luigi Zanutto (who published 'Fiore dei Liberi da Premariacco e i ludi e le festi marziali' in *Friuli nel Medio-evo* in 1907). Dr Ken Mondschein has published an excellent summary of Fiore's life based on the manuscripts and these two early 20th century sources in his book *The Knightly Art of Battle* and his open source (i.e. free!) article 'On the Art of Fighting: A Humanist Translation of Fiore dei Liberi's Flower of Battle Owned by Leonello D'Este'. I highly recommend both.

For our purposes, we are taking as read the idea that Fiore knew what he was talking about.

The four surviving copies of Fiore's manuscripts are:

Il Fior di Battaglia (MS Ludwig XV13), held in the J.P. Getty museum in Los Angeles. The 'Getty', as it is generally known, covers wrestling, dagger, dagger against sword, longsword, sword in armour, pollax, spear, lance on horseback, sword on horseback and wrestling on horseback. The text includes detailed instructions for the plays. It has recently been re-translated, with an extensive introduction, as *Flowers of Battle Volume 1*, by Tom Leoni and Gregory Mele, which is a must-have book for all Fiore scholars.

Flos Duellatorum is in private hands in Italy, and was published in facsimile in 1902 by Francesco Novati. The 'Novati' or the 'Pisani-Dossi' allows more or less the same order and has more or less the same content as the Getty. The main differences are that the spear section comes between the dagger and the sword, and the dagger against sword material is at the end. The text is generally far less specific than in the Getty, but it is the only version that is dated by the author, who states that he is writing on 10 February 1409 (1410 by modern reckoning).

Il Fior di Battaglia (Morgan MS M 383), the 'Morgan', held in the Pierpont Morgan museum in New York, proceeds more like a passage of arms: first comes mounted combat with lance, with sword, and unarmed; then on foot with spear, sword in armour, sword out of armour, and sword against dagger. There is no wrestling or dagger combat shown except against a sword, though they are mentioned in the introduction. I conclude that the manuscript is incomplete. Most of the specific plays shown here are also in the Getty, and these have almost identical texts.

Florius de Arte Luctandi (MSS LATIN 11269), recently discovered in the Bibliothèque Nationale de France in Paris, is probably a later copy. 'Florius' has Latin text and is beautifully coloured. It follows the approximate order of the Morgan, though is more complete, containing all the sections seen in the Getty and the Novati.

You can find scans of all of these manuscripts at the amazing Wiktenauer.com.

It is much easier when dealing with multiple versions of the same source to pick one as your main focus and refer to the others when necessary. Most scholars working on Fiore agree that the Getty is the most useful source, since it is as complete as any other, and has the fuller, more explanatory text. My goal in studying Fiore is primarily to understand how sword fights work. I am a martial artist first, historian second. From that perspective, it makes sense to focus on the most complete version of the book (which would rule out the Morgan), with the best illustrations and the most complete, explanatory text. The Getty is the only sensible choice.

The structure of Il Fior di Battaglia

Il Fior di Battaglia is a vast and complex treatise, covering an enormous range of weapon combinations, techniques, counters, and fundamental concepts. As it was written around 1400, it comes from a different cultural and educational background from ours, one in which memory training was fundamental. As a result, the lack of theoretical discussion in the work, and the way the information is presented, can present stumbling blocks to the modern reader. The sheer amount of information is daunting, and as it is spread over some 90-odd sides of vellum (conventionally numbered 1 to 47 recto and verso), keeping the structure clear in your head as you read can be difficult, so I'll lay it out for you. The first three written sides (p. 3 recto and verso, p. 4 recto) are taken up with a text-only introduction. This covers the following points:

- a brief autobiography of Fiore himself

- a list of his more famous students and some of their feats of arms

- a brief discussion of the secret nature of the art, and Fiore's opinions about different modes of combat (fighting armoured in the lists versus fighting in arming doublets with sharp swords)

- a further description of Fiore's training, and his opinions regarding the necessity of books in general for mastering the art

- a connection of Fiore himself and the book with a higher authority (Niccolò, Marquis of Este), who commissioned the work

- an overview of the book and its didactic conventions, beginning with some background information on wrestling, and advice to the student on what is required

- discussion of *poste* (the guard positions used in this art)

- a description of a crown and garter convention by which one can tell at a glance who is winning the fight in any given image.

This last is critically important to following what is going on in the treatise, so I'll expand on it here. The figures that begin each section are shown standing in guard, and wear a crown to indicate their masterly status. They are the 'first masters'. Following them are one or more 'remedy masters' (also called the 'second masters'), who illustrate a defence against an attack. Following each of them in turn are their scholars, identified by a garter, who execute the techniques that follow the previous master's remedy. After a scholar or master may come a 'counter-remedy master' (the 'third master') wearing a crown and a garter, who illustrates the counter to the remedy master, or to one of the remedy master's scholars. Occasionally, there is a fourth master, who may be called the 'counter-counter-remedy master', who wears the crown and garter too. Fiore specifies that most sequences don't get beyond the third master (i.e. the attack is met by the remedy, which the attacker counters), and it is perilous (perhaps because it is insecure) to go beyond three or four. This visual convention is unique to Fiore as far as we know, and makes it easy to be sure who is supposed to win from any illustrated position, and what stage of the fight (principle or guard; defence; counter to the defence; counter to the counter) is being shown. When reading the treatise, you can immediately identify who is winning in a given picture by his bling – the most bling wins!

The manuscript is divided into sections, which are linked together. The primary divisions (mentioned in the title of the Pisani-Dossi) are on foot, on horseback, in armour and out of armour. The secondary divisions are by weapon. We begin on foot, out of armour:

* *abrazare*: wrestling. This has one remedy master, and a total of 20 plays. The first 16 are unarmed, then come two with a short stick (*bastoncello*), and two with the stick against the dagger, connecting us to

* dagger: this is a huge section, with 76 plays, divided up amongst nine remedy masters. This is followed by defence of the dagger against the sword, and hence

* sword in one hand: this contains one remedy master followed by 11 plays, which will be detailed later in this book. They lead us to

* the sword in two hands: this starts with a description of footwork, then six different ways to hold and use the sword, then 12 guards. The plays are divided into
    * *zogho largo*, wide play: 20 plays, including two remedy masters
    * *zogho stretto*, close play: 23 plays deriving from a single remedy master, which is followed by
    * defence from sword guards on the left side – a single remedy master, with no scholars, who is followed by

* staff and dagger against spear, and two clubs and a dagger against spear. This seems to finish the unarmoured material (though some of the dagger plays require armour).

There follows:

* the *segno* page, or 'seven swords' – a memory map for the system as a whole, and illustrating the four virtues required for success in the art.

* From here on, we are mostly in armour:

* sword in armour – six guard positions, one remedy master, one counter-remedy master, and a total of 16 plays

* pollax – again six guard positions, eight plays with no specific remedy master, and two more showing variations on the axe: one with a weight on a rope, the other with a box of poison dust on the end. This is followed by the:

* spear – first we see three guards on the right, one play and one counter-remedy, then three guards on the left, and one play.

And finally, mounted combat:

* lance – five plays, each with their own master, including one counter-remedy

* lance against sword – five plays, including three counter-remedies

* sword – one guard position, shown against two attacks, with nine plays

* *abrazare* – seven plays including three counter-remedies

* on foot with *ghiaverina*, a type of spear, against mounted opponents, one master followed by two plays

* lance and rope – a last play of lance against lance, showing a specific trick for dismounting an opponent

* sword against sword – a last, probably allegorical, play, in which you chase your opponent back to his castle, in which his villainous friends are waiting.

The sections complement and reinforce each other: when a longsword pommel strike comes in, treat it like a dagger attack: when you end up too close to use your pollax, use the wrestling plays. There is much to learn about the spear from the plays of the sword, and so on.

In any given section there will usually be one or more remedy masters wearing a crown, illustrating the defence against a particular attack. These are followed by scholars, wearing a garter, who complete the play of the previous master. There are often also counter-remedy masters, wearing a crown and a garter, which counter either the scholar that comes before them, or the master himself. In other words their action may be specific to one scholar, or more generally applicable to the remedy itself.

The plays are the illustrations of the techniques, so we see a picture of a player (wearing no crown or garter) getting beaten by a master, scholar, or counter-remedy master. One technical sequence, such as a parry and strike, might take up one, two or three such illustrations, each of which is a play. As the term implies, there is often a lot of 'play' in the execution of these techniques, and several different ways to enter into a given play. Fiore scholars tend to keep the key plays in memory, in the order that they appear in the Getty MS It has become the norm to refer to the plays by their number – such as 'the third play of the second master of *zogho largo*'. This is more useful than saying 'p. 25 verso, bottom left illustration', because it puts the play into its context. It is also how Fiore himself refers to the plays. In this numbering system, the illustration showing the master is the first play, and all the images that follow him, up to the next master, are numbered two, three, etc. This makes it very easy to find the play referred to – simply find the right master (wearing a crown and no garter), and count from there.

Equipment

Don't worry, you don't need garters or crowns to practise. All you will need at this level are:

* A fencing mask.

* A training dagger. A 30 cm length of dowel will do – ideally with a bunch of tape on one end, or a rubber blunt, to minimise injuries if you make a mistake.

* A training longsword. A wooden waster is fine, and really at this stage you could make do with a 120 cm/four-foot-long stick. As with the dagger, a bit of padding on the end in case of mistakes is a good idea. If you are using a blunt steel sword, it should have a rubber blunt on the end – it makes a great deal of difference to the likelihood of puncture injuries.

That's it. We will discuss more sophisticated equipment when you need it.

Using this workbook

I have divided the course material in this book into four classes of about 90 minutes each. You may well find that without a live instructor there you may need more time to go through the material. It is better to go slower and really get to grips with the material you are working on, than to try to cram too much material into the allotted time. Please treat the division into classes as a suggestion, not a rule! And you may well want to go over the same class several times before moving on. Go at your own pace.

It is very important that you clearly distinguish between blocked practice and play. In blocked practice you will set up a drill choreographically, and practise it as accurately as you can. This is an essential starting point – it teaches you *what to practise*. By itself though, it isn't really practice at all. For that we have many approaches, the most important of which is play. I introduce play in the very first class, and you will be learning how to play usefully throughout this course. Just be advised that 'play' does not equal 'do what the hell you like'. Every game has rules, and to use the games effectively, you must pay attention to those rules and play within them. For a detailed breakdown of how to develop skill, there's a whole chapter on it in *The Theory and Practice of Historical Martial Arts*, and we will apply those principles in the next workbook in this series.

I have organised the material here based on what I have found works best for most groups of students. For instance, we are not taking the material in the order that Fiore presents it in the Getty and Pisani-Dossi manuscripts. If you want to take it that way, there is a second table of contents at the beginning of the book that will help you find all the *abrazare*, then dagger, then sword plays, in the order they appear in the Getty manuscript.

Time

Every action has a beginning and an end – we measure the action by the time it takes to get from one to the other. Any counter to the action must occur at the correct point along that timeline. For example, my opponent tries to hit me on the head. I want to knock their blow aside and hit them. If I parry before they strike, my action fails. If I try to parry after they strike, forget it, they've already hit me. If I parry during their strike, it may work. We can in theory divide their strike into an infinite number of tiny units of time, but in practice, we can act against their blow at the following times:

1. before it starts – we can prevent it ever happening

2. as it leaves its starting point

3. as it is about half way to the target (probably my head!)

4. just before it reaches the target

5. as it passes the target (this requires us to have avoided the blow).

The correct time to parry is either 3 or 4; to start a counterattack, 2, to attack, 1, to avoid anywhere between 2 and 4, to strike after a parry, 4 or 5 (depending on whether the blow was parried at point 3 or 4).

Fiore's art makes most use of point three, with a firm parry after the attack is committed, but long before it lands.

Time also refers to the initiation of an action: which bit moves first? In almost all cases, the weapon should move first. Specifically, the point of the sword should move first. I will go into this in more detail when we discuss striking, but a mental image from the German tradition, to be found in Ms. 3227a (aka 'The Nuremburg Hausbuch') sums it up nicely: strike as if you had a piece of string tied to the point of your sword, and it was pulled suddenly into the target. This means your sword travels in the shortest possible line, as direct and fast as can be.

Measure

All fencing actions have their proper measure: the distance at which they are supposed to work. The position of the sword determines the length of the strike itself: how far the sword point has to travel from where it is to where it is going. The position of your feet and weight relative to the target determine how far you need to step during that motion of the sword to strike.

With the longsword we take both the motion of the sword and the footwork into account when determining measure, but as a general rule, measure is described according to what the feet have to do to accomplish your goal. As you approach your opponent you are in one of these positions:

- Out of measure: it will take more than one step to strike.

- In wide measure you can hit with your longest attack using a single foot movement. With the longsword this is a passing step.

- In close measure you can hit without stepping.

- Once inside the reach of the sword, you need to grapple; so let's call it grappling measure.

At any given time, your opponent will also be in one or other of these measures. Depending on the angle of approach, your reach, and the lengths of your swords, one of you may well be in (for instance) wide measure while the other is out of measure.

The ideal position to be in is such that you can strike without stepping, while your opponent has to step to strike.

Structure and flow

Good structure is the foundation upon which all martial skill is based, and is the fundamental skill behind great feats of apparently magical ability. In short, it is as simple as making sure that for whatever you want to do, every bone in your body (there are over 200) is in exactly the right place, and every muscle (there are over 600) has exactly the right degree of tension. This takes some practice, but it is easy to acquire major technical improvement with relatively little work, by minimising the unnecessary tension that inhibits your movement.

No matter what your structure, it will be stable in some directions, unstable in others, with a specific pattern of strength and weakness. Martial skill comes from making sure that you move from a strong position that does not inhibit your movement, through a succession of equally supported positions into your final position, with no resistance from unnecessary tension, so the work being done by your muscles is all available for creating the movement. And this movement is directed into your opponent's structure in a way that exploits to the full the pattern of strength and weakness in their position.

Let us take a simple example: stand with your feet apart, pointed in the same direction as you are facing. Have a friend gently press from the side against one shoulder – you should find it easy enough to direct that pressure into the ground through the opposite foot. Then have him apply the same gentle pressure into the centre of your chest, directly across the line between your feet. As you have no leg in that direction, you will either fall, or be forced to take a step to support yourself. In other words, you have to change your structure to adapt to the pressure.

Human beings are bipods: as any photographer could tell you, bipods are inherently unstable, which is why cameras are used with tripods. Imagine your opponent as a tripod – where would the third leg go? Any pressure in the direction of the imaginary third leg will be much more effective at destabilising them than pressure directed into either one of his actual legs. We call this direction the 'line of weakness', and the specific spot where the third leg should be, the 'triangle point'. Of course, that third leg could be in front or behind; the line connecting those two points is another way of conceiving of the line of weakness. As you move, you should be aware of your changing lines of strength and weakness. Naturally, it is ideal if your strikes are made in the line of your strength, directed into the line of your opponent's weakness.

It is important that you grasp the idea that every position has an ideal structure, which you work to attain, and your and your opponent's positions have lines of strength and weakness which you must apply and exploit. In general, where possible, apply your strength to their weakness – if their line is stronger, change your structure.

One of the hallmarks of good structure in a martial arts position is that it allows the techniques that are supposed to work from there to flow easily from it. I consider structure and flow as the fundamental elements of basic training.

Flow is the single most difficult aspect of this art to describe on the page. It encompasses speed and power generation, and is experienced as freedom of movement. Good technique should flow effortlessly from and through your perfectly structured guard positions. If your actions fail to flow, you should fix your structure. If your structure is wrong, you probably moved into it wrong: you failed to flow. As we saw above, any position is a combination of the position of your bones and the pattern of tension in your muscles. How you get into that position determines the pattern of muscular tension within it, and therefore determine in part what can be done from there. Normally, a strong, clean movement will create a more useful end structure than a sticky, awkward one.

Every defence you make will be done against an opponent who is moving in some way (attacks are sometimes done against a stationary opponent). Your defence will interrupt their movement, but by itself that may not be enough. If they can simply flow around your defence and strike, then the technique will fail. You break their flow if you simultaneously interrupt their movement and interfere with his structure.

You can destroy your opponent by breaking their structure, or by interrupting their flow. If you successfully maintain your structure and flow, you cannot fail. Nothing breaks structure and interrupts flow quite like a blade to the head!

As a general rule, good movement creates good structure, which easily generates good movement. In short:

Flow creates structure, structure enables flow.

How to parry

You're going to be doing quite a bit of sword-on-sword work in this workbook, so here's the theory about how that works.

The usual approach to parrying in Fiore's system is to beat the incoming attack away with your sword. The blades meet middle to middle – you literally aim to cut the attacking sword away with the middle of your blade.

The primary goal of a parry is to beat aside the incoming attack, allowing you to strike safely. A parry works by using a line of stability in the defending sword to exploit a line of instability in the attacking sword, and imparting momentum to the incoming sword.

The sword itself is mechanically strong in the plane of the edge, and weak in the plane of the flat. Usually when the sword is extended, the edges are supported by the bones of the forearm, which are literally pointing in the same direction. The triangle formed by your arms is supporting the edge. However, there is practically nothing supporting the flats – there is no no bone in that direction. So, when trying to control the opponent's sword, where possible use your edge against their flat. This also minimises damage to your edge if you are using sharp swords (if you need this book, you should not yet be doing drills with sharps – put them away and go get your blunts!).

THE FIRST CLASS

In this first class we will cover some basic guards, strikes, and defences with the dagger, and some basic sword handling. It will all be done very gently, but it is still a good idea to have a thorough warm-up before we start, which serves several functions. Firstly, it prepares you for the specific actions of the style, and secondly, it allows the instructor to see all the students move, which tells them a great deal about what he or she needs to teach you about how to do various actions.

Warm up, first class
https://guywindsor.net/aw1001

Fiore uses guard positions (poste), steps, and turns (volte) to define movement. Every guard position has a set of offensive and defensive characteristics, and every action can be thought of as moving from one position to another, with one of the turns or steps.

The four guards of *abrazare*

Fiore's art begins with four guards. This should come as no surprise, as four is the standard number for building a base with. These four guards are:

- *Posta longa*: long position, both arms extended, but one forwards and one back (think: grab her throat).

- *Posta di dente di zenghiaro*: the guard of the wild boar's tusk: arms are bent at the elbow, with the forward hand thrusting up (think: break her jaw).

- *Posta di porta di ferro*: the guard of the iron door, both hands down (think: throw her head on the ground).

- *Posta frontale*: frontal position, both hands up and forwards (think: thumbs in eyes).

For our purposes, these guards are most usefully thought of as the fundamental waypoints of every movement. If I wish to stab you in the face with my dagger, which is on my belt, and both my hands are down, I go from hands down (*porta di ferro*), draw my dagger up (*dente di zenghiaro*), and stab you, extending the arm (*posta longa*). You might defend yourself by attacking me while I'm still in *porta di ferro*; entering as my hand rises into *zenghiaro*, or by intercepting my hand as it goes towards *longa*. Any later and you are hit, unless you get out of the way.

For now, just pass forwards with each guard, with this mnemonic:

Grab her throat,
Break her jaw,
Thumbs in eyes,
Head on floor.

Four guards
https://guywindsor.net/aw1002

The four steps

Fiore says there are four things in the art: *passare, tornare, accrescere* and *discrescere*. These are generally understood to mean to pass forwards (*passare*) or back (*tornare*), or to step keeping the same foot in front, forwards (*accrescere*) or back (*discrescere*).

These actions can be made in any direction, though we usually describe eight: forwards, backwards, right, left, diagonally forwards right and left, diagonally backwards right and left. Forwards describes the direct line between you and your opponent. For now let's keep things going in a straight line.

Four steps
https://guywindsor.net/aw1003

Notes

(Include information like: the dates of your practices, any actions that were particularly difficult, or felt particularly helpful, links to additional resources. Ideally you will have a complete record of your progress.)

Grips, strikes, and breaks

In this system there are two ways to hold the rondel dagger, four ways to strike with it, and two ways to break an arm. Before we move on to the attacks and defences that make up Fiore's plays, it's worth separating these skills out and spending some time understanding them.

Gripping the dagger:
The dagger can be held either way up in your hand: point up, like a tennis racket, or point down, like an ice pick.

It is a good idea to practise switching between these grips, with either hand, to develop dexterity.

Dagger dexterity drill

1. Hold the dagger point down.

2. Slip your index ring and little fingers off and around the grip.

3. Flip the point up and bring your forefinger over the grip. Dagger is now point up.

4. Take your forefinger over the guard.

5. Flip the point down and bring your thumb around to catch the handle.

6. Bring your fingers around to grip. Dagger is point down again.

Repeat!

Dagger dexterity drill
https://guywindsor.net/aw1004

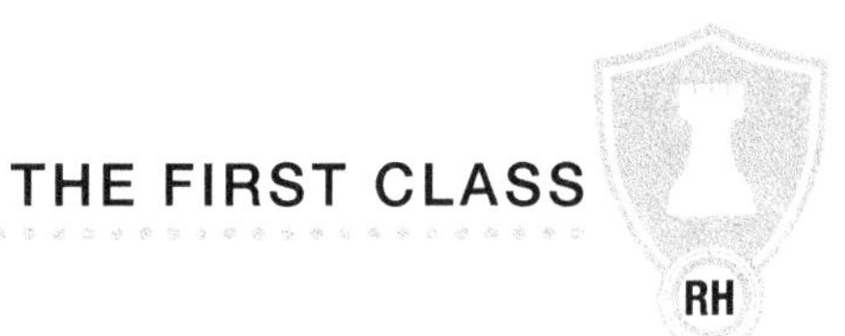

Notes

Dagger blows

There is not a single cut or slash in any of the 76 plays Fiore gives us. He calls the strikes *colpi* (blows), and shows us four lines to strike in.

1. *Fendente*: straight down, to the top of the head and as far down as the elbow.

2. *Mandritto*: forehand, to the temple, and as far down as the elbow

3. *Roverso*: backhand, to the temple, and as far down as the elbow

4. *Sottano*: up the middle, no higher than the chest.

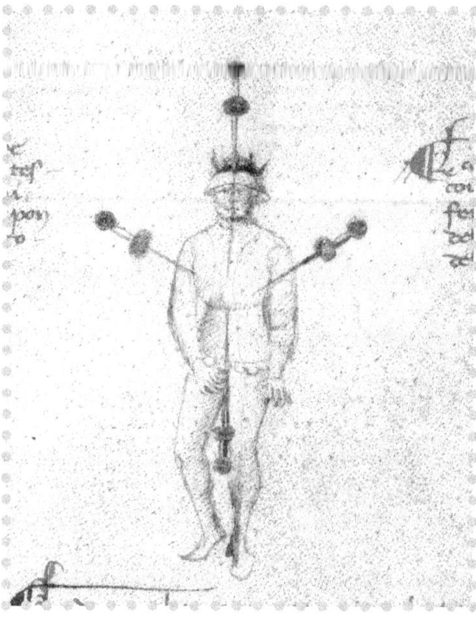

Note! The middle blow is usually called *sottano*, low, by modern practitioners, though Fiore himself does not ascribe a formal name to it. He does say that the *roversi* blows (and by implication the *mandritti* also) are called *mezani* (middle). He also points out that striking forehand or from below is safer than backhand because the left hand can be used to cover yourself as you go in.

You should practise these blows on your own to the air, and to striking targets such as a reinforced punch bag. Go through them all in order (say, 10 *fendenti*, 10 *mandritti*, etc.) then build up combinations such as *mandritto, roverso, mandritto*. Use your imagination!

Dagger blows
https://guywindsor.net/aw1005

Notes

First master, first play (disarm)

The next step is to strike at your partner. You both put masks on, just in case, and take turns passing in with a *mandritto* dagger strike, just touching the mask.

Once that is comfortable, we have established the central problem in martial arts: somebody is trying to hit you. What should you do?

The first solution Fiore gives us is to take their weapon away and stab them with it. Like so:

1. Attacker and defender both in *porta di ferro*, left foot forwards.

2. Attacker passes to strike with a *fendente*, aiming at the mask.

3. Intercept the attacker's wrist with your left hand while stepping diagonally back, and

4. Turn it to the left, creating a leverage disarm with the dagger against the back of your wrist.

5. Collect the dagger and strike.

This is the first play of the first master of the dagger.

Assuming a right-handed attacker, the weapon is coming to your left side. So using your left hand reaches further, and taking the step back diagonally right gives you more time to do the action.

Dagger first master disarm
https://guywindsor.net/aw1006

Once the basic choreography is comfortable, it's useful to define the window of opportunity. With any martial arts technique, there is a finite time, determined by your opponent's actions, in which the technique will work. Too early or too late, and it fails. People don't usually stop dead and wait for you to finish what you're doing. To keep things simple and approachable, the attacker will continue their motion by extending their non-dagger hand to your mask, passing forwards. You need to move away enough, and do the technique quickly enough, to get it done before their hand touches your face.

Notes

Now what?

You have rightfully attacked, your partner has taken your dagger away and stabbed you.

There are two ways we can go from here: we can look at how you would counter that disarm, or we can try a disarm against a different attack.

Both are good options, so choose which one feels more right to you and your partner right now. At this stage in a beginners' class, I'll usually demonstrate both options briefly, and then get the class to vote on what comes next.

Or you can do both, if you're not limited for time.

First master, second play: the counter to the disarm

As your partner intercepts your wrist, you're going to turn your dagger from forehand to backhand, and stab them in the chest (gently!).

Dagger first master counter to the disarm
https://guywindsor.net/aw1007

Notes

Disarm against the roverso (third master)

This action comes from the Pisani-Dossi manuscript, where it is the first and second plays of the third master of dagger. It looks like a lot to do, but in practice is quite smooth and easy. You can of course just do a mirror-image version of the first play of the first master, and not worry about wrapping their arm so they can't escape.

1. Attacker strikes *roverso*, aimed at the mask.

2. Intercept the strike with your right hand, stepping your left foot to the left.

3. Turn the dagger clockwise and…

4. Grab the dagger with your left hand, stepping in with your left foot behind the attacker's right, and…

5. Collect the attacker's elbow under your left armpit, locking the arm and…

6. Strip the dagger out of the attacker's hand, and…

7. Wrap your left arm around the the attacker's right arm and…

8. Take the dagger with your right hand and strike under the attacker's right arm.

When the basic choreography is clear, the attacker should indicate the closing window of opportunity with the touch on the mask, as before.

Dagger third master disarm
https://guywindsor.net/aw1008

Notes

Holding the sword, and shoulder swings

This is the moment most students have been waiting for: holding the sword. The first thing I teach in my salle is how to get the swords safely off the wall racks without stabbing anyone by accident. Most people reading this won't be training in a salle like that, but however your swords are stored, make sure they are pointed *down* unless you are very sure there is space to swing them. It's better to accidentally poke someone in the foot than the eye.

Your dominant hand goes near the crossguard. Your other hand goes on the pommel. Relax your grip. We will work on the specifics of how to hold the sword when you have a way to apply the differences; for now, this will do. Let's start with some gentle swings.

Stand still with your feet apart, your sword on one shoulder, and swing your sword to the other without thinking too much about it. Occupy your thinking mind with noticing what the blow feels like. Let the first blow swing forwards with enough relaxed vigour that it ends up swinging around to your opposite shoulder (so if it started on the right, it finishes on the left). Right now, I don't care about starting position, ending position, accuracy or anything else, except that the movement be comfortable and easy. Do it as fast or slow as you like.

Sword swings
https://guywindsor.net/aw1009

Notes

If you are nicely relaxed, you'll notice that as you swing the sword your body wants to follow it, your hips turning, and perhaps the heel of your back foot (the one on the side where the sword started) coming off the ground. Let that happen.

As you swing from side to side, notice the point at which the paths would cross. Usually for most students it's near the ground, as with a golf swing. Direct it to about head height. Keep the movement gentle.

Once this is comfortable, as you swing from the right allow the swing to pull you into a passing step forwards with your right foot. When you swing back from the left, allow that to create a passing step with the left foot.

Sword Swings with step
https://guywindsor.net/aw1010

Notes

Mandritto fendente, roverso fendente

Now that you have the movement going, let's adjust it. Imagine you have a paintbrush on the end of the sword, and are painting lines on a wall in front of you. Let the lines look like this:

Place an imaginary person in front of you, and slice them from the left side of their jaw to the right knee, and the right side of their jaw to their left knee.

These blows are called *fendente*. You do them either forehand (*mandritto*) or backhand (*roverso*).

Mandritto and *roverso fendente*
https://guywindsor.net/aw1011

Notes

If you take these blows slowly, you will have time to notice some of Fiore's guards spontaneously appearing as you move. For a right hander, starting on the right shoulder:

You're beginning in a forward-weighted *posta di donna destra,* throwing the sword forwards to *posta longa,* (that's a *mandritto fendente,* a forehand descending blow) letting it fall so the pommel touches your left hip in *posta di dente di zenghiaro:*

Then bringing it up to the left shoulder in *posta di donna la sinestra*, striking again (this time with a *roverso fendente*, a backhand descending blow) into *posta longa* (with your left foot forwards), letting the sword fall until the pommel touches your left hip again in *tutta porta di ferro*, letting it pass back to *posta di coda longa*, and back up to *posta di donna destra*.

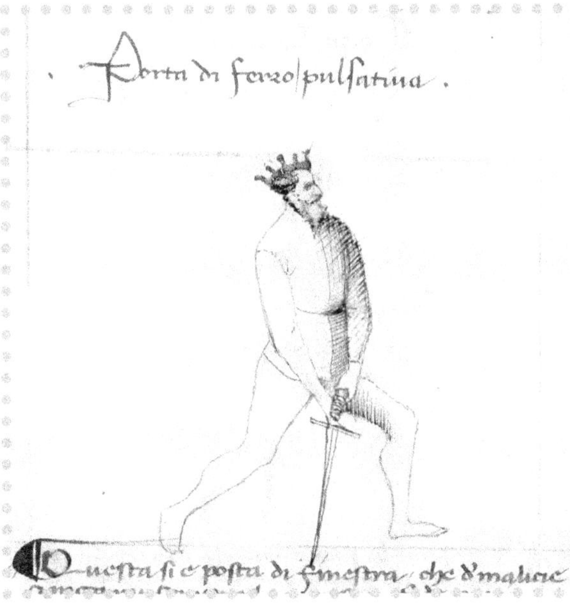

For a left hander, you'd start in *posta di donna la sinestra*, throw your *mandritto fendente* to *longa*, through to *dente di zenghiaro*, up to *posta di donna destra*, throw your *roverso fendente* to *tutta porta di ferro*, through to *coda longa*, and up to *donna la sinestra*.

You may notice that Fiore's illustrations show some of these guards as rear-weighted positions. For now, you will be doing all of them forward weighted, because it's easier for beginners. This is canonical because Fiore states that all guards can do a *volta stabile*, which shifts your weight from one foot to the other. Don't worry about it for now.

You don't need to worry about the terminology at this stage. Just notice how the blows create the guards, and how every guard is the beginning, middle, or end of a blow.

Fendenti creating guards
https://guywindsor.net/aw1012

Notes

THE SECOND CLASS

The second class includes lots of revision from the first class. This doesn't make a lot of sense from a book perspective, so I'll just include references to the repeated material rather than writing it all out again. We will also cover basic falling practice, some more in-depth footwork, some more dagger plays, and your first longsword pair drill.

Warm up

Warm-up, second class
https://guywindsor.net/aw1013

Falling

To practise the dagger plays and wrestling plays properly, you must know how to fall safely. That's a skill to be developed slowly over time – and there's no time like the present.

One crucial skill that you will need for safely training the close-quarter work – or just if you live somewhere where they have ice on the streets in winter, or indeed if you think it likely that at some point between now and when you die you will fall over and don't want it to hurt – is falling safely on a hard surface.

If you are training to fight on a padded surface (such as in judo or wrestling) then training using mats makes sense. Also, when you get to the level when it is safe to train in killer throws (where you drop your opponent on his head, for example), mats may be needed for your partner's benefit. However, using the method outlined here, I have taught all my students to fall safely on our nice smooth concrete floor (no broken glass! No rocks! Luxury!), at least

sufficiently well that takedowns can be done to the ground. It is critically important that you take it gently to start with and remember:

NO PAIN

If it hurts, you're doing it wrong! Stop!

Our basic objectives are to minimise impact, and absorb what little impact there is through pads of muscle. Your bones should never touch the ground: it hurts! The reason we must avoid pain is because if we experience falling as painful, our bodies tense up and we start to fall even worse because we are flinching in anticipation of the pain. So limit yourself to 3–5 minutes of falling practice in every session until it's so comfortable you scarcely need bother practising it.

Note that I am not expecting your falling to reach the level where you can simply flip out of any lock or roll away from any attack – that kind of skill absolutely requires training under the direct supervision of a qualified instructor. This is just to get you to a level where if your partner is in position to throw you, they can and you won't be injured by it. Also, I am leaving out any consideration of the fight continuing if you are thrown because in medieval contexts, as a general rule, if you have fallen you will either die anyway, or have lost the bout, and also because Fiore does not cover ground fighting at all.

Let's start on the floor and work up. This first exercise looks a bit like a sit-up, but is absolutely not supposed to be trained like one.

The starfish

1. Begin by sitting on the floor, leg wide and straight.

2. Place your right hand on or near your left foot.

3. Smoothly roll back down along your left side,

4. Until you are flat on the floor (this is the starfish), then

5. Roll back up along your right side to place your left hand on your right foot.

6. Roll back along your right side, back to the starfish position and

7. Continue from step one…

Crucial points:

• Your spine must not touch the ground. Avoid bone to floor contact at all times.

• The motion should feel like rolling, effortless and graceful.

• If your feet come off the floor as your shoulders come up, it's because your hips and lower abdomen are too tight. Relax!

Getting up again: roll and up

Gravity will get you down to the ground: the tricky bit is getting back up again. The critical skill here is getting your feet under your hips. The easiest way I know to do this is to fold one foot underneath you, and throw the other one over and forwards, using the momentum of the leg and foot to pull your hips up and over the tucked-in leg. We call this exercise 'roll and up':

1. Start in a kneeling position, left foot forwards.

2. Roll back on your left side (just like in a starfish).

3. Swing your legs up in the air, to gather some momentum.

4. Bring your left foot in to your bum.

5. Throw your right foot forwards, at about 90 degrees to your left shin.

6. As your right foot hits the floor, push your hips up and over your left foot.

7. From here you could stand up quite easily – but let's keep going…

8. Roll back on your right side.

9. Let your feet swing up.

10. Bring your right foot in to your bum.

11. Throw your left foot forwards.

12. As your left foot hits the floor, push your hips up and over your right foot.

13. And keep going from step one!

Getting to the floor

So, now you can get back up elegantly and gracefully, let's have a look at getting down. As before, let's start close to the ground. Most beginners start this from a seated kneeling position. Cross your arms over your chest, so they will not be used to break your fall (which from standing may break your wrist), nor will your elbows bash the ground (which hurts from any height). You should not use your hands to get down or back up for the simple reason that this is a martial art, and your hands should be busy holding your sword, grabbing a dagger out of your opponent's belt and sticking it in her femoral artery, or finding something else useful to do. So, whatever's going on, they are far too busy to be used for simply falling.

From this kneeling position, just drop to one side. You should arrive in a sort of rolling motion, from hip to upper arm to shoulder. Zero impact! Then get back into position without using your hands and repeat in the other side. This gets easier with practice.

Then, when that is comfortable (today, tomorrow, in a week or a month), bring one foot up and repeat.

Then, when that is comfortable (no rush), bring your weight up a bit.

And work your way up to a full standing position.

At any stage here, you can use a partner to push you gently, showing you where and when to fall. This makes it quite a bit harder to do, especially if they choose an awkward direction.

So, you can get from standing, to lying on the ground, when and where your partner requires, without using your hands and with no pain of any kind. This is the point of falling practice.

The video here is longer than usual, as it's a short class on safe falling.

Learning to fall safely
https://guywindsor.net/aw1014

Notes

Footwork revision

Memory is a skill, and must be trained like any other. At this stage you should do all the footwork stuff you remember. Do NOT check back to get reminders: recognition and recollection are two very different processes. We're working on recollection. Go through it for two solid minutes.

Done?

Did you remember the four steps? Passing forwards and backwards, and stepping forwards and backwards?

Let's add the three turns.

The three turns

Fiore defines three turns, stable, half, and full. The stable turn is when both feet stay in place and you can play on the same side in front or behind; the half turn is when with a pass forwards or backwards you can play on the other side; the full turn is when one foot stays in place and the other turns around it.

When executing the stable turn (*volta stabile*), it is essential that you unify your forces – every part of the body is moving in the same direction. The turn is about 135°, and it often helps to use the unarmed *posta longa* or *posta frontale* to establish direction.

The half turn (*mezza volta*) is at one level just a pass (see above) backwards or forwards. It is stated in the text that you can play on the other side, so it is reasonable to infer that it may be accompanied by a rotation of the hips. I interpret the addition 'in front and behind' to refer to the direction of the pass.

The whole turn (*tutta volta*) is wide open to interpretation. Strictly speaking, any time one foot turns around the other, in any direction or any distance, it's a tutta volta. In practice, it is used as either an adjusting step to align yourself with the *strada* (the line between you and your opponent), or a way to apply force in some joint locks and throws.

It's a good idea to practise these turns on their own and in sequence, until you are familiar with the actions and the terminology.

The three turns
https://guywindsor.net/aw1015

Notes

The four guards drill

In my salle, most basic-level Fiore classes begin with the 'four guards exercise', which has you combine the four guards with the three turns. It is a specific reference to our main source, a familiar starting point (once you know it), and a way to get into the proper way of moving without distraction. It goes like this:

1. Start in *posta longa*, right hand and foot forwards (because this is how it is shown in the treatise).

2. Establish the line you will walk along – if you are indoors, make it parallel to one wall.

3. Leading with your left hand, *volta stabile into longa on the left.*

4. Leading with your right hand, *volta stabile* back to where you started.

5. Leading with the left hand, *mezza volta* to *posta longa* on the left, along the *strada.*

6. Leading with the right hand, *volta stabile* into *zenghiaro.*

7. Leading with the left hand, *volta stabile* into *zenghiaro.*

8. Leading with the right hand, *mezza* volta into *zenghiaro.*

9. Leading with both hands, *volta stabile* into *frontale.*

10. Leading with both hands, *volta stabile* into *porta di ferro.*

11. Leading with both hands, *mezza volta* into *frontale.*

12. Leading with both hands, *volta stabile* into *porta di ferro.*

13. You can now *volta stabile* into *longa* on the left side, and…

14. Repeat everything the other way around.

When you run out of space, in either direction, use a *tutta volta* to turn yourself around, elegantly and in style, into the next guard of the sequence and continue.

The four guards drill
https://guywindsor.net/aw1016

Notes

Dagger revision

In the previous class you did the first play of the first master of the dagger, and either its counter or the first play of the third master. Or possibly both. Grab your daggers and put your masks on, and see what you can remember.

Having done that, try the one you missed out.

Now do them all again, and see if you can improve your ability to do the disarms by adjusting your direction, considering the triangle point.

Counter to the third master disarm

Once you've done both, let's have a look at the counter to the third master disarm. This is really fun.

Fiore shows us one counter-remedy to the third master in the Pisani-Dossi MS:

1. Strike a *roverso*, aimed at your partner's mask.

2. They intercept the strike with their right hand, stepping their left foot to the left.

3. Trap their right wrist with the dagger, reaching underneath your own right arm with your left hand to grab it near the point, and uses the trap to drive their elbow towards their triangle point.

The third master disarm counter
https://guywindsor.net/aw1017

Notes

Sword or dagger?

At this point you're either hooked on dagger and want to do more or eager to get on to the sword stuff. So choose. We can do a disarm against a *sottano* dagger blow, or get on with a fancy sword handling drill. Take your pick!

The ninth master disarm

Strictly speaking, we should grab the attacker's wrist with both hands, then shift our right hand onto the dagger, but in practice if you know this is coming, it's easier to go straight for the dagger as described below. Purists, feel free to do it canonically.

1. Attacker and defender left foot forwards.

2. Attacker passes in to strike with a *sottano*, holding the dagger in a forehand grip.

3. Catch his wrist with your left hand, dagger blade with your right and…

4. Lift your left hand, levering the dagger forward and down with the right and…

5. Stab the attacker in the chest.

When the basic choreography is clear, the attacker should indicate the closing window of opportunity with the touch on the mask, as before.

The ninth master disarm
https://guywindsor.net/aw1018

Notes

The six grips handling drill

Fiore shows six distinct ways of holding the longsword on these pages:

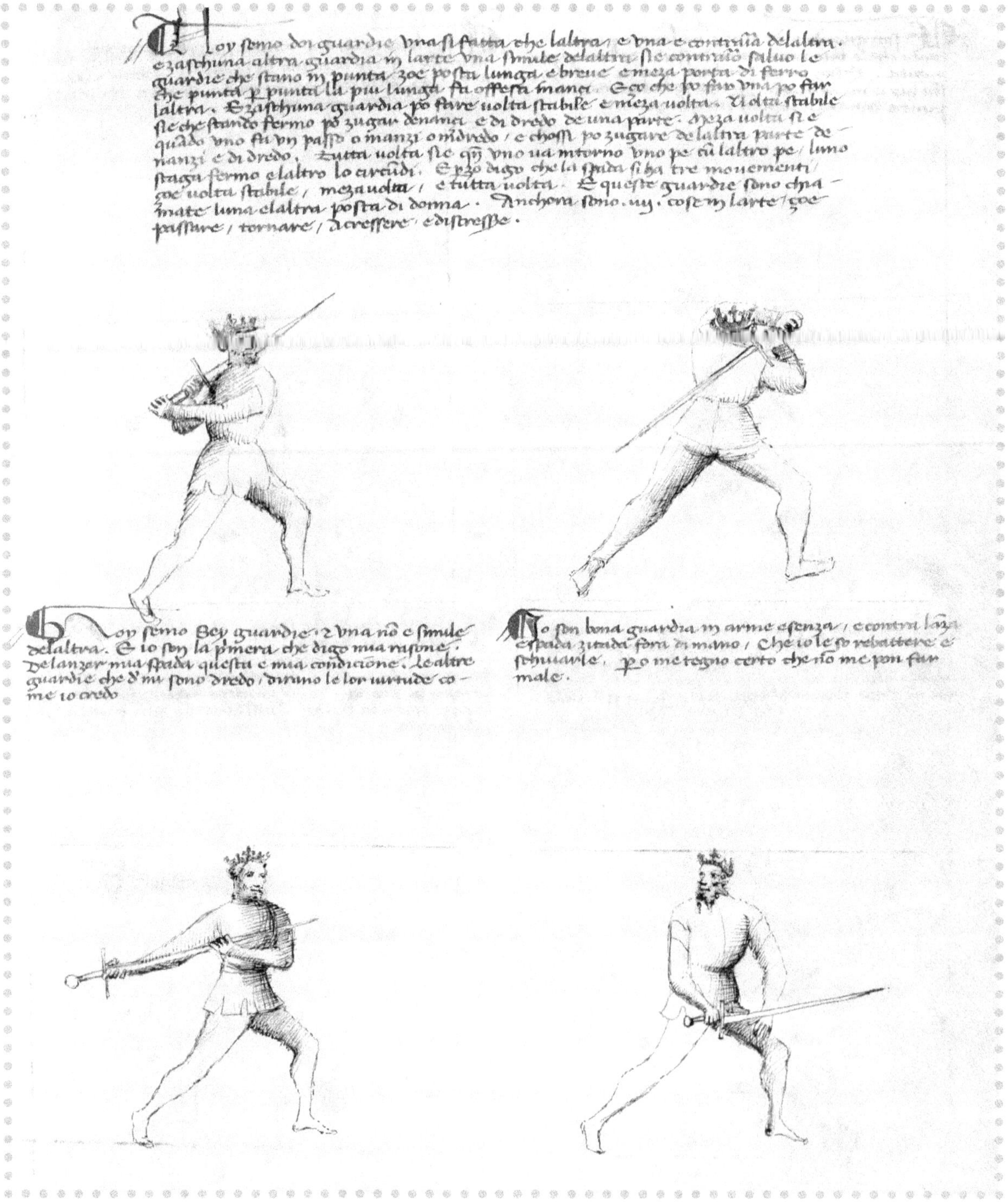

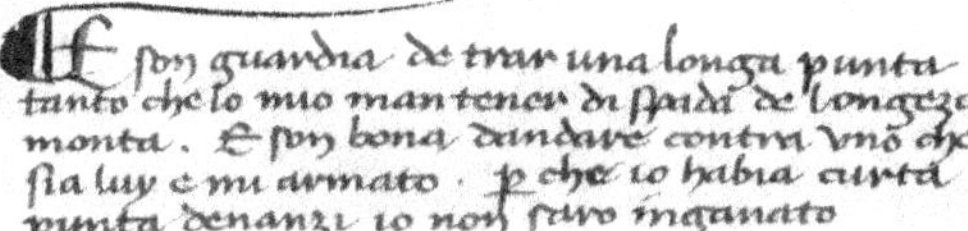

Io son guardia de trar una longa punta
tanto che lo mio mantener di spada de longeza
monta . E son bona dandare contra vno che
sia luy e mi armato . p che io habia curta
punta denanzi io non saro inganato

Io son bona guardia contra spada azza e daga siando
armado . p che io tegno la spada cu la man mancha
al mozo . Ello fac̄o p fare contra la daga che me po
fare de le altre arme pezo .

Guardia e posta di donna son chiamata
p che cu queste altre prese de spada e son dun
spada . che una no e tal presa che laltra, ben
che questa che me contra mi pare la mia guada
se no fosse forma d'azza che la spada si mtada .

Questa spada sic spada e azza . Egli grandi pesi
gli lieieri forte inpaza . Questa anchora posta de
roma la soprana , che cu le soi malicie le altre guar
die spesso magana , p che tu crederai che traga de colpo
io traro di punta . Io no ho altro a fare che leuar gli
brazzi sopra la testa . E posso buttar vna punta, che
io lo presta .

Switching between them in a playful way will speed up your ability to control the weapon.

The grips are:

1. to throw the sword

2. sword in one hand

3. by the pommel for a long thrust

4. half-sword

5. the 'normal' grip

6. by the blade like an axe.

We start by switching from normal grip to half sword, back and forth.

Then take the blade hand off and hold the sword by just the pommel for a long thrust.

Then we play with reversing the grip, as if to throw, and then we add holding the sword like an axe.

The six grips handling drill
https://guywindsor.net/aw1019

Notes

Revising your blows

Without referring to the book, go through the sword-swinging we did in the last class. It doesn't matter if you don't remember the names of the blows and the guards at this stage.

If you get stuck, then skip back and revise a bit. Don't move on to the next thing until you're comfortable with the two named blows.

Learning to stop

Power is nothing without control. Would you buy a car that had an accelerator but no brakes? Before we start doing pair drills with the sword, you need to be able to stop the blow. At the gentle pace we are going, it shouldn't be very difficult.

Just pause a moment in *posta longa* when you do the actions.

So, make your strikes, but let them stop in the extended position. If that's hard, you need to slow right down. Don't move on to pair drills until this is easy: your partner's health depends on your skill.

Pausing in *longa*
https://guywindsor.net/aw1020

2

Notes

Parry and strike

So, let us set up our first defensive drill. Remember, masks on, common sense engaged! It is critically important that you can trust your partner, and that they have developed sufficient control of the weapon that they can throw a gentle, slow, but accurate and in-measure blow to just stroke the mask as if it was made of eggshell. If you have any doubts about your or your partner's ability to do this safely, then go to the "pell" exercises in the eighth class and practise them to develop control.

In principle every cut can be an attack, a parry, a counterattack (where you parry and strike in one motion), or a feint. To start with we are going to use *mandritto fendente* to parry an attack of *mandritto fendente,* and then strike, as we see in these images:

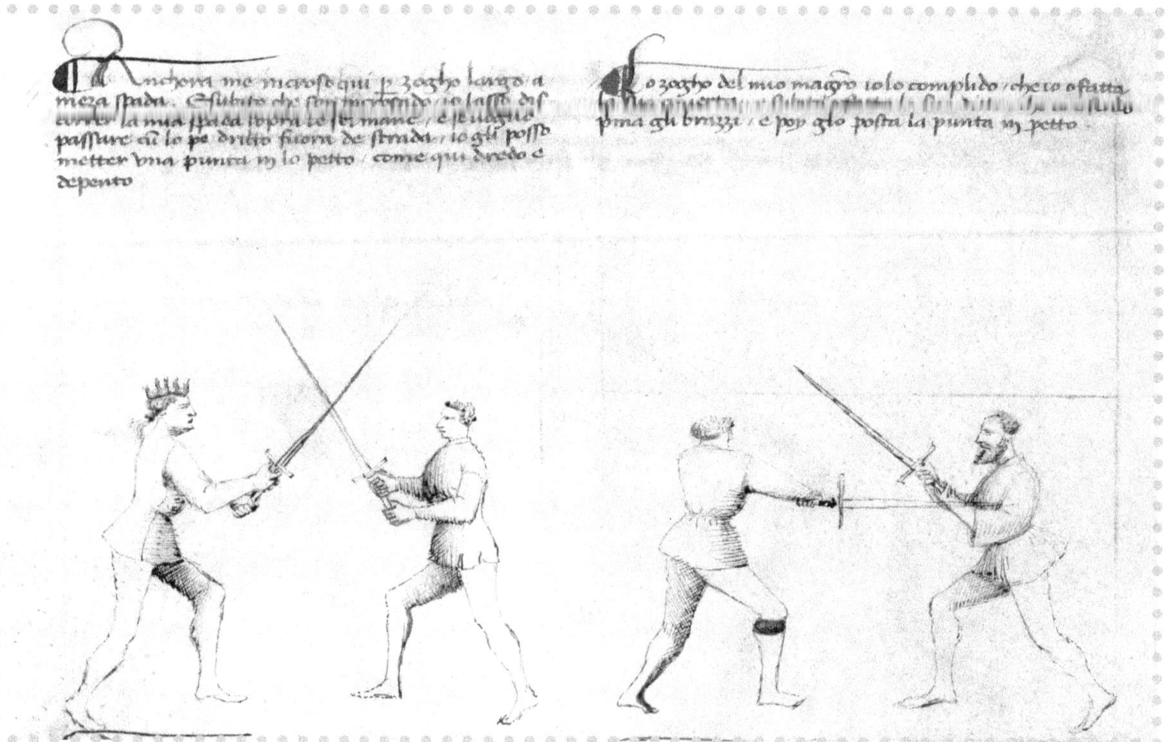

1.   You both start in *posta di donna destra.*

2.   Your partner throws a gentle blow, touching your mask.

3.   That's the set-up. Now, when your partner throws that same blow again:

4.   Parry with your own *mandritto fendente,* aimed so that you cut the middle of their blade with the middle of yours. Go gently to start with.

5.   That beats their weapon aside, and you can step to your right, and gently cut their head.

This is a version of the first and second plays of the second master of the *zogho largo,* in which after the parry you would cut their left arm and then stab their chest. We will leave that until you have a bit more experience.

Notes

2

Note for cross-handed pairs: it is much easier if you begin right v. right, or left v. left, whichever handedness you have. This means that one or other of you may be attacking, or parrying, with a *roverso*. That's fine.

When practising steps one and two, the attacker should not just throw the *mandritto fendente* and stop dead. Instead, gently touch the defender's mask with the *fendente*, then gently poke them in the stomach, and step back out of measure. Get used to every attack including multiple strikes, and a recovery out of measure. Go very gently.

Parry and strike
https://guywindsor.net/aw1021

Notes

THE THIRD CLASS

The class begins with a warm-up as usual. It is a good idea by this stage if you are able to warm yourself up without being led, but feel free to use the warm-up videos if you like.

I like to segue from the warm-up into falling practice, by including the starfish, going from there to roll and up, and then a bit of falling practice.

From there, go through your four steps, three turns, and the four guards drill. See if you can do it without checking back. Spend a couple of minutes on this, then check to see how accurately you remembered it.

The first two plays of abrazare

The four guards begin the section on *abrazare*, wrestling. So let's continue with the first two plays of wrestling, which are the master and his first scholar.

It's important at this stage that we do it exactly as it's shown in the manuscript, because there are lessons embedded in the plays that only become clear if you're doing them as shown.

1. Stand right foot forwards.

2. Your partner puts their left hand on your right shoulder, and has their right hand ready as if to punch you in the stomach.

3. Find their left elbow with your right hand, and their right elbow with your left hand. You are opposing their extended arm with your bent one, and their bent one with your extended one.

4. Trap their left hand between your right shoulder and your right cheek, and use your right forearm near the elbow to drive their elbow to your left, with a *volta stabile*.

Fiore shows stepping through, to drop and break the elbow, but keep both your feet on the ground and go very gently. Elbows are delicate!

The keys to getting this to work nicely are hyperextending your partner's elbow, and pressing it in the correct direction.

The first two plays of *abrazare*
https://guywindsor.net/aw1022

Notes

The third play of abrazare

This is a really interesting moment in the source, because Fiore explicitly tells us to change what we're doing based on our opponent's actions. He says that if they take their hand off your shoulder, you should throw them on their back, instead of forwards onto their face. When practising this, do NOT let your partner fall, unless they are trained to fall this way, which has not been covered in this book as it's much more advanced.

Here's how we do it:

1. Set up as for the first two plays.

2. As you apply pressure to your partner's elbow, they drop their elbow, bending their arm.

3. Extend your hand (gently!) to their right cheek, and turn them to your right.

4. *Accrescere* forwards and to your right, which will increase the throwing force, so be careful.

5. As their left foot comes up off the ground, catch under their knee with your left hand. Be careful to have stepped offline, or their foot will come up into your groin.

Notice that the direction you're moving in is on the same line as for the second play, just in the opposite direction.

The third play of *abrazare*
https://guywindsor.net/aw1023

Notes

How did you like wrestling? OK, that wasn't really wrestling, it was a gentle go at one specific wrestling technique. There are 20 of them in this section of the manuscript, but we'll only cover six of them in this workbook, so you're halfway through.

From here, we can go on to the next wrestling play, or move on to the dagger plays. You choose!

Notes

The fourth play of abrazare

This play covers the problem of your opponent having the 'wrong' leg forward. Because of this, their line of weakness will change from your front right/back left, to front left/back right.

1. Set up as for the first two plays, but your partner has their right foot forwards and is closer.

2. Their right hand goes to your left hip, your left hand goes over their elbow and grabs the back of their right hip.

3. Their left hand is round the back of your neck. Your right hand goes to their left cheek.

4. Push diagonally left with your right hand, and turn to your right to destabilise them.

Fourth play of *abrazare*
https://guywindsor.net/aw1024

The wrestling story so far goes like this: control their elbows. Break their arm by turning into their line of weakness. If their elbow isn't available take their head. If their feet are the other way round, go to the other diagonal.

Do you see why I want you to be really precise about which foot is forwards?

Notes

Dagger revision

Begin with the dagger handling drill, and revise the four strikes. Then gently with your partner go through the dagger plays that you know. This includes the first master disarm and its counter, the third master disarm and its counter.

If you didn't do the ninth master disarm yet, go learn that. You'll need it for the next drill.

The Dagger disarm flowdrill

A flowdrill combines several actions together in a circular fashion – one action counters the next, and so on. They are a standard training component of most martial arts I've come across. This flowdrill combines three disarms into a continuous flow.

1. Begin with your partner attacking you with a *mandritto*. Disarm them, and strike a *roverso* towards the right side of their mask.

2. They intercept that with the third master's disarm, and strike a *sottano* to your belly.

3. You counter that with the ninth master disarm, and strike a *mandritto* to their mask.

4. They counter that with the first master disarm, and so on.

Step as needed to get where you need to go, and look for a flowing, co-operative drill at least until you can both do it smoothly. This drill will become a base for practising other techniques.

The dagger disarm flowdrill
https://guywindsor.net/aw1025

Notes

How to practice pair drills: the rule of Cs

You learn the art of arms from the people you train with, and your companions will learn it from you. To learn anything, you need a clear idea of what you are trying to learn, and a feedback mechanism for telling you whether it's working. In martial arts training, your feedback mechanism is usually your partner.

To begin with, you will be co-operating in getting the choreography of the drill correct. Spend as much time as you need to get the basic idea working: you do A, I do B, then C happens. This is what you have done in this book so far.

But don't stay there a minute longer than you have to. The next stage, where you will spend most of your training time, is for one of you to coach the other.

The final stage, which you won't get to in this book, is to compete with each other.

Let's take the first play of the first master of the dagger as an example.

Your partner attacks; you intercept their wrist and take their weapon away, then hit them. When figuring out the choreography, you go very slowly, and can stop and change your feet, or fiddle about with your grip on their wrist, and so on.

Once that's clear, you already have a mechanism for improving this: your partner keeps moving forwards, to touch your mask with their other hand. This puts some pressure on you to do the same action, but better. That's the essence of coaching.

You can also do the drill as a competition, such that they just try to hit you, and you try to defend yourself. If they hit you they win; if you get control of the dagger you win. This very quickly becomes very dangerous, so avoid this for now.

I call this way of categorising your training approaches the 'rule of Cs': choreography, coaching, competition.

From now on, once the choreography is established, you should be coaching each other. Here's how:

1. Be very clear who is coaching whom. At any given iteration of the drill, there is only one coach.

2. Be very clear what they are coaching you to do. Get better at the disarm? Get better at the strike after the disarm? Get better at the footwork? The more specific the better.

3. Success = the student hits the coach. Failure = the student's action fails, and the coach hits them.

4. The coach adjusts the intensity such that the student gets to succeed about eight times in ten. This is the *optimal rate of failure*. If the student is succeeding too often, they are not learning. Up the intensity. If they are failing too often, ease off a bit.

5. Every step of every pair drill can and should be coached.

Coaching can absolutely be done playfully. Yes, it's a formal training environment, but play is about the fastest way to learn anything. Just keep the play safe, and within the general bounds of the drill you're trying to work on.

Notes

There will be times in the future if you take the art very seriously when training will be frightening, dangerous, and challenge you to your very core. But that's not something to worry about now, and not a healthy attitude to take at this level. Training can and should be *fun*.

Notes

Sword handling and striking revision

Now take up the sword and practise the solo exercises you remember.

If you haven't done the six grips handling drill, go back and do that.

Up, down, around, around

I've used this basic handling drill since I founded my school. It will teach you to manipulate the sword more precisely, and introduces the rising blows.

1. Begin in a relaxed *posta longa*.

2. Leaving the hands forward bring your point back towards your shoulder.

3. Cut forwards with a *mandritto fendente* to *posta longa*.

4. Drop the point and sweep the sword round in a circle on your right side, cutting *mandritto fendente* to *posta longa*.

5. Bring the point back towards your shoulder but let it sweep round in a circle on your right side, cutting up with the true edge, your hands rising until they are above head height, and pushed forwards.

6. Repeat on the other side.

You will notice that it is very different on the other side, especially in the rising blow, because your hands will either cross (with a *roverso*) or not (with a *mandritto*). With the rising blows, allow your hips to turn to support the movement.

You can also try this drill with just one hand, using the arm as little as possible.

Up, down, around, around
https://guywindsor.net/aw1026

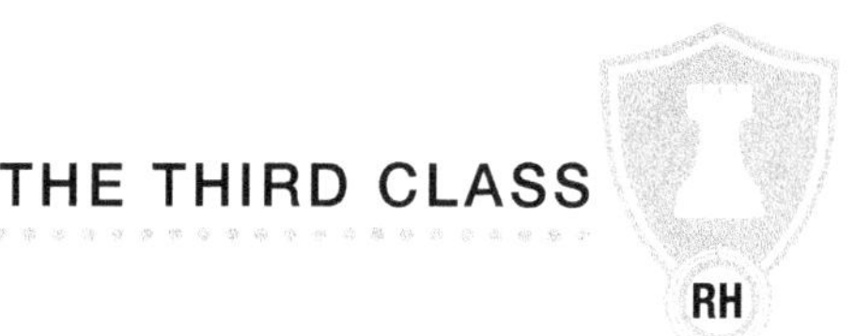

Notes

The cutting drill, part one

This is a handy drill for memorising the most used strikes, and for getting you to strike from the low guards. Don't worry about part two yet, it's a lot more advanced.

1. Begin in *posta di donna destra*, left foot forwards.

2. Cut a full *mandritto fendente* through *posta longa* to *dente di zenghiaro*, passing.

3. Cut *roverso sottano* to *posta longa*, with the false edge, passing. This can also be done as a thrust – it looks almost identical.

4. Go to *posta di donna destra* (no step).

5. Cut a *mandritto fendente* to *posta longa*, passing.

6. Go to *posta di donna la sinistra* (no step, you're just moving the sword).

7. Cut a full *roverso fendente* to *tutta porta di ferro*, passing.

8. Cut *mandritto sottano* to *posta longa*, false edge, passing. This can also be done as a thrust.

9. Go to *donna la sinistra* (no step).

10. Cut a half *roverso fendente* to *posta longa*, passing.

11. Bring the sword back to *posta di donna destra* (no step), and you're back where you started. So, do it again!

The cutting drill, part one
https://guywindsor.net/aw1027

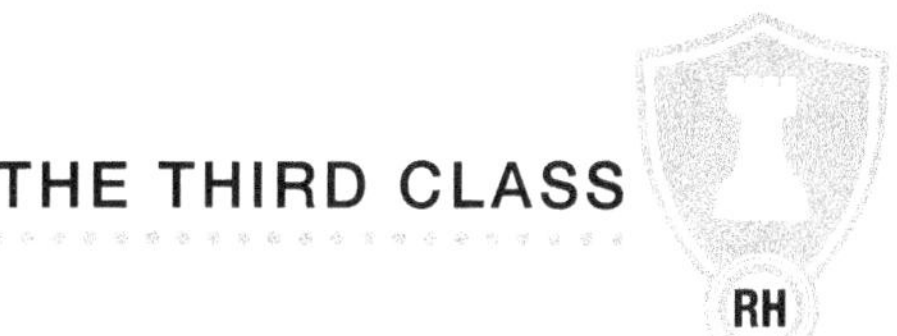

Notes

First drill revision

Set up the first pair drill, where you parried a *mandritto fendente* with a *mandritto fendente*. Get that comfortable, and we'll move on.

Remember that at step one, the attack, the attacker should touch the mask, thrust at the belly, and recover out of measure.

OK, now you have a choice: we can either discover the attacker's counter to that parry (go to 'first drill, step three'), or we see how to defend from a different starting point (skip ahead to 'second drill, steps one and two').

First drill, step three: pommel strike

Set up as for first drill, then as you attack:

1. Your partner parries. Allow the point of your sword to be beaten wide. Keeping your sword hand up and forwards, allow that momentum to turn your sword around, creating a natural cover against their strike, and presenting your pommel forwards.

2. Pass in immediately, using your other hand to control their closest elbow and strike their mask (gently!) with your pommel.

First drill, step three: pommel strike
https://guywindsor.net/aw1028

Notes

Parrying from the low guards

You may not be conveniently in *posta di donna destra* when your opponent attacks. You need to be able to defend from whatever position you happen to be in. Let's start building that skill by parrying from *tutta porta di ferro*.

1. You are in *porta di ferro*.

2. Your partner attacks with a gentle *mandritto fendente*.

3. Cut up at their sword, aiming to cut the middle of their blade with your true edge, beating it (gently) aside, and cut gently to their mask, passing to your right as before.

If you are interested in an in-depth academic discussion of why we do this action this way, see pages 219–231 in *From Medieval Manuscript to Modern Practice*, which is also available as a free article 'One Drill, One Play, Many Questions' here: https://guywindsor.net/onedrill

Parrying from *tutta porta di ferro*
https://guywindsor.net/aw1029

Notes

Parrying from dente di zenghiaro (second drill, steps one and two)

What happens if we change sides? Parrying from *dente di zenghiaro* is described in detail by Fiore, so we'll do it by the book. The key difference here is we are parrying with the false edge (so there's no need to turn the sword), and we are stepping to the right (for right-handers) with an *accrescere*.

1. You are in *dente di zenghiaro*.

2. Your partner attacks with a gentle *mandritto fendente*.

3. Make sure to include some reps where you don't do anything, just let your partner practise their attack. They should then touch your mask with the *fendente*, come back to the mask with a gentle thrust stepping to their left, and cut again with a *roverso fendente*, while passing back to their diagonal left, to get safely out of measure.

4. Once your partner has practised that a few times, then as they attack with that first *mandritto fendente*.

5. Cut up at their sword, aiming to cut the middle of their blade with your false edge, beating it (gently) aside, stepping to your right with an *accrescere*, and cut gently to their mask.

Parrying from *dente di zenghiaro*
https://guywindsor.net/aw1030

Notes

THE FOURTH CLASS

Begin with a warm-up, about 10 minutes. Make sure you include falling practice. Then five minutes of footwork, including the four guards drill.

At this stage, choose whether you're going to go over your dagger drills, or do *abrazare* instead.

If you chose *abrazare*, skip ahead a page; if you chose the dagger, read on.

Start with a couple of minutes of dagger manipulation and strikes.

Then go through the three disarms that you know and the two counters.

I bet you want to know the counter to the ninth master disarm, right?

Here it is:

Ninth master dagger disarm

Set up the drill to practise the ninth master's disarm, and go through it a couple of times.

Once that's comfortable, when your partner grabs your wrist and the dagger blade, reach over with your other hand and grab the point of the dagger. Use this extra leverage to twist it free. Fiore describes this in the text on folio 18 verso of the Getty manuscript (the back side of page 18), but doesn't give us an image to go with it.

Ninth master disarm counter
https://guywindsor.net/aw1031

Now run through the dagger disarm flowdrill. One of the three disarms will be the least comfortable, so spend a few minutes working on that. Then put it back into the flowdrill.

Once that is comfortable, set up the flowdrill and break the flow by taking it in turns to execute the counter to the disarm. You get to pick which disarm you'll counter, and there's no need to inform your partner of which one you'll do! Go gently though.

If you chose abrazare

You already know plays one two and three; you may have skipped number four. If so, run through 1–3, briefly, then go back and cover the fourth.

Spend a few minutes on 1–4, paying attention to the lesson embedded there.

Now let's look at plays five and six.

The fifth play of abrazare

In plays one to three, the player has their left foot forwards, you have your right. In the fourth play, the player has switched legs. Now in the fifth, we look at the problem of the player having their left foot forwards again (so the line of weakness will be back where it was in the first three plays), but they have both hands round your waist. What should you do?

Following the example of the third and fourth plays, you know that if the elbow is unavailable, you go to the face. So, with your left hand gripping their right hip, press your right hand to their left cheek, turning their head, and twist them to your right.

Notes

The sixth play of abrazare

Set up the fifth play. As your partner makes contact with your face with their right hand, catch their right elbow with your left hand and push it up. That will turn them off their base.

Notes

The sixth play of *Abrazare*
https://guywindsor.net/aw1033

This is the first counter-remedy shown in the manuscript, so it's probably quite important. Fiore says to push the elbow 'of the hand that offends your face'. Looking at the images, we see that in the fifth play, the scholar is using his right hand to push the face, but here in the sixth, the scholar is pushing the player's *left* elbow. So it's not actually possible to go perfectly by the images.

Notice that this play, the counter-remedy, is basically the same idea as the second play – push the elbow. You might also notice that you are continually using your bent, *dente di zenghiaro*/boar's tooth arm to control their extended, *posta longa*/long guard arm.

Notes

The great advantage to including dagger drills this early in your training is that the weapon is not a challenge to control. This means you can very quickly incorporate flowdrills, coaching, and other more advanced training concepts. This keeps your tactical senses alive and develop your ability to train while you bring your longsword handling up to the point that you can meaningfully move beyond the choreographical stage.

So, please run through the following:

- the six grips handling drill

- the up-down-around-around handling drill

- the cutting drill (part one).

Once that's done, mask up and go through as much of First Drill as you know (that's either the first two steps, or first three), and parrying from the low guards (*tutta porta di ferro* and *dente di zenghiaro*). Whichever option you skipped last time, go back and do now.

Now let's add the defender's counter to the pommel strike at step 3 of first drill.

First drill, complete

Happily, Fiore provides a specific counter-counter remedy to this pommel strike, in the ninth play of the master of *coda longa* on horseback, in which as the pommel strike comes in, he simply raises his sword to deflect it and executes a pommel strike himself.

So, set up first drill, steps 1-3.

1. As you parry and the point of the attacker's sword is beaten wide, they enter with the pommel strike, and…

2. Your strike after the parry fails against the attacker's cover, so…

3. As their pommel strike comes in, lift your hands, directing the attack off to the side, and strike the attacker in the face (also gently!).

A cross-handed pair will find that there should be the opportunity for the attacker to wrap the arms, but the normal counter to a wrap as shown above in the first set of drills doesn't work quite right here. So instead, step out of the way and push the attacker's sword up and away with your off-hand.

First drill, complete
https://guywindsor.net/aw1034

Notes

By this stage you have some experience of the system, and no doubt some favourite parts. Maybe dagger drills are your jam, maybe longsword handling drills. You must become competent at all of the parts before you will be really good at any one of them, but that is some way away, so for now, feel free to choose which of the next two classes you want to do first.

The fifth class will establish through a specific example how dagger training complements longsword. We'll take a basic dagger technique, practise it a couple of different ways, then see how that applies to a longsword problem.

The sixth class covers two fundamental longsword plays that you haven't seen yet: the break and the exchange.

Take your pick!

4

Notes

THE FIFTH CLASS

Warm up as usual, include the falling practice, and go through the four guards drill. When that's comfortable, get into a dagger frame of mind with the four strikes and the dagger disarm flowdrill.

We are going to have a look at the third and fourth plays of the first master, which involve cranking the arm. The fifth and sixth plays have the same basic mechanics but are easier for every beginner I've ever trained to do, so we will cover those first. Before we get on to that, let's have a brief look at how arm locks work.

In general, we focus on the elbow joint. If your partner's arm is straight, we make it too straight, by applying pressure on the wrist and elbow in opposite directions. This is a hyperextension, also known as an arm-bar. It can be done in any direction, but we will usually push the elbow up, in an over-the-shoulder break, or down, as you have done in the second play of the *abrazare*.

If their elbow is bent, we turn it relative to the shoulder, in either direction. In effect, we use the forearm as a lever, the upper arm as an axle, and crank it around to dislocate the shoulder. (Don't actually dislocate it!)

In both cases we need a lever (the forearm) a fulcrum (the elbow) and the correct direction in which to apply force, which will always be away from their hips and towards the imaginary third leg (the triangle point).

Arm lock mechanics
https://guywindsor.net/aw1035

First master of dagger, fifth play

Let's have a look at the crank in action, in the fifth play of the first master.

1. You are both in *porta di ferro*, left foot forwards.

2. Your partner passes to strike with a *fendente*, aiming at the mask.

3. Intercept their wrist with your left hand and their elbow with your right…

4. Cranking the wrist around the elbow while stepping away – usually with a *discrescere* back right.

This is a brutal and quick arm break, so be careful. As soon as the choreography is clear, add the attacker's hand-to-mask continuation and start coaching.

First master, fifth play
https://guywindsor.net/aw1036

Notes

First master, sixth play

This counters the fifth play, by reinforcing the striking hand and redirecting the attack.

Be very sure to have a good fat blunt on your dagger, as it's going somewhere delicate.

The counter is an essay in simplicity – as the defender's right arm comes forward, grip your dagger by the blade with your left hand and stab them in the elbow, like so:

1. Set up the previous drill, and

2. As your partner intercepts your wrist with their left hand and your elbow with their right…

3. Grab the dagger blade with your left hand and place it in the crook of their right elbow.

4. Apply pressure down and to the right, unbalancing them (and if the daggers were sharp, destroying their elbow joint).

This is an excellent example of a general rule in this system – when in doubt, shove their elbow.

First master, sixth play
https://guywindsor.net/aw1037

Notes

First master, third play

This is the famous *ligadura mezana*, middle lock, which appears in many places in the manuscript. Mechanically it's basically the same as the fifth play, but instead of getting a hand on the wrist and a hand on the elbow, you use your elbow on their wrist and your wrist on their elbow.

Next, we use one arm to bind the attacker's weapon, leaving the other free to hit them. We can also turn the lock into a break or a throw. It is probable given the illustration (which shows the attacker's dagger on the ground under the defender's foot) that the lock follows the disarm. However, I find it easier for beginners to do this as their first option, and it is also more useful when translating this material to the sword to treat turning their wrist to disarm and wrapping their arms as two separate things.

1. You are both in *porta di ferro*, left foot forwards.

2. Your partner passes to strike with a *fendente*, aiming at the mask.

3. You intercept their wrist with your left hand and

4. Slip your hand down to their elbow…

Notes

5.   Finding their wrist with your own elbow…

6.   And turn their arm anti-clockwise parallel to the line of weakness to break their structure, driving their elbow towards the triangle point in front of them, and their wrist towards the triangle point behind them.

This leaves them vulnerable to all sorts of nastiness, not least the following:

- Hit them in the face.

- *Volta stabile* to your right to take them down.

- *Tutta volta* to dislocate their arm.

One common problem with this technique is your partner straightening their arm. This is a safety issue, as by straightening their arm it becomes hyper-extended earlier than when you are expecting the technique to end, and so injury may occur. In effect, we have an arm-bar instead of a crank. Be careful and co-operative at this stage, but as soon as the choreography is clear, add the attacker's hand-to-mask continuation as usual.

First master, third play
https://guywindsor.net/aw1038

Notes

First master, fourth play

This is the famous *ligadura sottana*, lower lock, which appears in many places in the manuscript. Mechanically it's basically similar to the sixth play, but instead of getting a hand on your dagger, you grab your own wrist, and mechanically attack their left elbow.

- Set up as for the previous play.

- As your partner slips their hand towards your elbow, turn the point of your dagger away from them…

- And grab your right wrist with your left hand…

- Collecting their elbow with your right wrist…

- And turn to your left driving their elbow towards their triangle point.

Turning the point of the dagger makes all the difference – it changes the mechanical structure of your elbow, making it much more resistant to their technique.

You must also turn your hips into your line of weakness to stabilise yourself against the locking pressure. This happens naturally if you are reaching over with your left hand, but bears mentioning.

Be careful, as this is a brutally effective lock that can easily dislocate the shoulder or elbow.

First master, fourth play
https://guywindsor.net/aw1039

Notes

Now switch to longswords, and go through the handling drills and cutting drill. Get comfortable with the weapon. Once that's in place, mask up and go through the basic pair drills that you know – first drill, and parrying from the low *guards tutta porta di ferro* and *dente di zenghiaro*.

Keep it relaxed for now.

Pay special attention to the first step of each drill, the attack. Make sure the attacker is stepping in with the first strike, and getting back out of measure again with other strikes.

In first drill, it's just *mandritto fendente* with a pass forwards, thrust to the belly then pass back.

In second drill, it's *mandritto fendente* with the pass forwards, thrust to the mask with a pass to the attacker's left, and *roverso fendente* to the mask bringing your right foot round behind you, then pass back. I've included steps one and two of second drill in the next video.

Notes

Second drill, step three

This drill begins with the attack of *mandritto fendente*, parried from *dente di zenghiaro*.

1. As you attack and your partner parries, stepping offline, turn your sword hand to keep your sword in the way of theirs, keeping your hand high.

2. Let go of the sword with your left hand and pass in with your left foot...

3. Finding their right elbow with your left hand and enveloping it, with the same mechanics as for the *ligadura mezana*.

4. You are now in control of their arms, their sword, and their balance. Strike gently to the mask with your pommel.

Fiore would have us thrust to the face here, but one-handed thrusts while your other arm is busy are challenging for most beginners to control, so we go with the safer pommel strike.

Second drill, steps one to three
https://guywindsor.net/aw1040

Notes

Second drill, step four

In this step of the drill, we apply the same basic counter to the *ligadura mezana* as you have already seen in the fourth and sixth plays of the first master of the dagger. You will regain control of your weapon by turning it and grabbing the point, and use that very long lever to very carefully apply the *ligadura sottana* to your partner's elbow.

1. Set up the drill as before. As your partner covers your *fendente* and comes in to wrap your arms…

2. Turn your pommel away to your right, bringing your point towards your left shoulder…

3. Grab your blade with your left hand…

4. And gently turn to your left, locking their arm.

Second drill, step four
https://guywindsor.net/aw1041

Notes

THE SIXTH CLASS

This class will cover the two basic thrusting plays Fiore shows us in the *zogho largo* section. We will also look at the seventh play of the first master of the dagger, because it's somewhat related.

Warm up as usual, include falling, and run through the four guards drill.

Then run through the dagger disarm flowdrill. Notice how as you play, you naturally adjust your feet to adjust your measure and structure to get the results you want.

Now let's take a look at the seventh play.

First master, seventh play

This introduces the takedown. Fiore tells us that there are five things you need to know to do with the dagger: to disarm, to strike (we've covered those), to lock (third play, which you may not have done yet), to break the arm (fifth play, which you may not have done yet), and to throw them to the ground, which you have flirted with in the *abrazare* plays.

The essence of any throw or takedown is to remove your partner's hips from the base they are resting on. This is usually done by twisting them off their feet. I have modified this play for safety. As Fiore describes it, the attacker should not be getting up again.

Set up as for the first play and then:

1. Intercept your partner's wrist with your left hand, turning it to the left while…

2. Stepping out of the way with the right foot (away from the attack) while…

3. Placing your right hand on your partner's left shoulder, and…

4. Keeping your right arm extended, pass diagonally left with your right foot (if needed, you can add more force with a volta stabile once the pass is complete.)

5. Your partner will fall on their left side. Maintain control of the weapon at all times.

This is an excellent opportunity to make use of your painlessly acquired falling skills.

Correct placement of your legs prevents them from turning their hips (and stepping) to keep their hips over their feet, so down they go. If your partner is not ready to fall yet, just go to the point where they are at the edge of their balance and stop.

First master, seventh play
https://guywindsor.net/aw1042

Once that throw is comfortable as written, try this variation: as the attack comes in, instead of stepping back towards your rear left, *acrescere fora di strada* (step out of the way), to the left with your left foot, into the attack, pushing it away from you. In the same movement, your right hand goes to their shoulder.

This is more difficult, because you have less time to do it in, and more dangerous because if you get it wrong you'll get hit, and if you get it right you'll destabilise your partner much earlier.

Now move on to longsword revision – handling drills, cutting drill, and pair drills that you already know. In the cutting drill pay special attention to the thrust from *tutta porta di ferro* to *posta longa*, and from *dente di zenghiaro* to *posta longa*.

Done? Let's add the next new thing: the exchange of thrusts (*scambiare di punta*). This is the ninth and tenth play of the *zogho largo*.

Notes

The exchange of the thrust

1. You wait in *tutta porta di ferro*. Your partner is in the same guard.

2. They thrust to your stomach.

3. Pick up your point and cross their sword (middle to middle, edge to flat) – your hands stay low.

4. Step your front (left) foot out of the way (to the left – this pushes their point further away from you)…

5. And pass across (so, diagonally left), thrusting to his face (no need to lift your hands: keep them low!).

If this is done smoothly, it feels like a simple strike that happens to collect his attack. But beware – it is critically important to make sure of your cover before passing in. Otherwise you eat steel – very embarrassing.

Fiore, fount of all wisdom that he is, kindly provides for the possibility that your thrust might miss, and in the next play has us pass again (with the left foot, same direction) while reaching over with our left hand to grab the opponent's sword between their hands, and strike. I always include this – if you don't miss, no problem, you get them twice. If you have missed, the continuation is automatic.

Exchange of the thrust
https://guywindsor.net/aw1043

Notes

Breaking the thrust

If we suspect that the thrust may be too strong to exchange safely against, for instance because it begins on the attacker's left side and so must be pushed all the way across our centre, we must then commit to a much stronger defence, and beat their thrust to the ground.

The mechanics for this action are implied in Fiore's instructions: "catch his sword with a *fendente*, with your hands above and point below..." I do this by keeping my pommel in place to start with, and rotate the sword around it, catching the incoming sword, then throwing the point forward and left with the *accrescere*, following with the pass to step on the sword. It is definitely correct to step on their blade (Fiore shows it), but for our purposes, and to save on new swords when ours get bent or broken, it is OK to step just short of their point (Fiore also shows this). In either case, the beating down action must have finished before your passing foot arrives. You should try to throw their sword into the ground. From here you can strike, as Fiore instructs, "with the false edge, to the throat under his beard, returning with a *fendente* to the head or arms" thus:

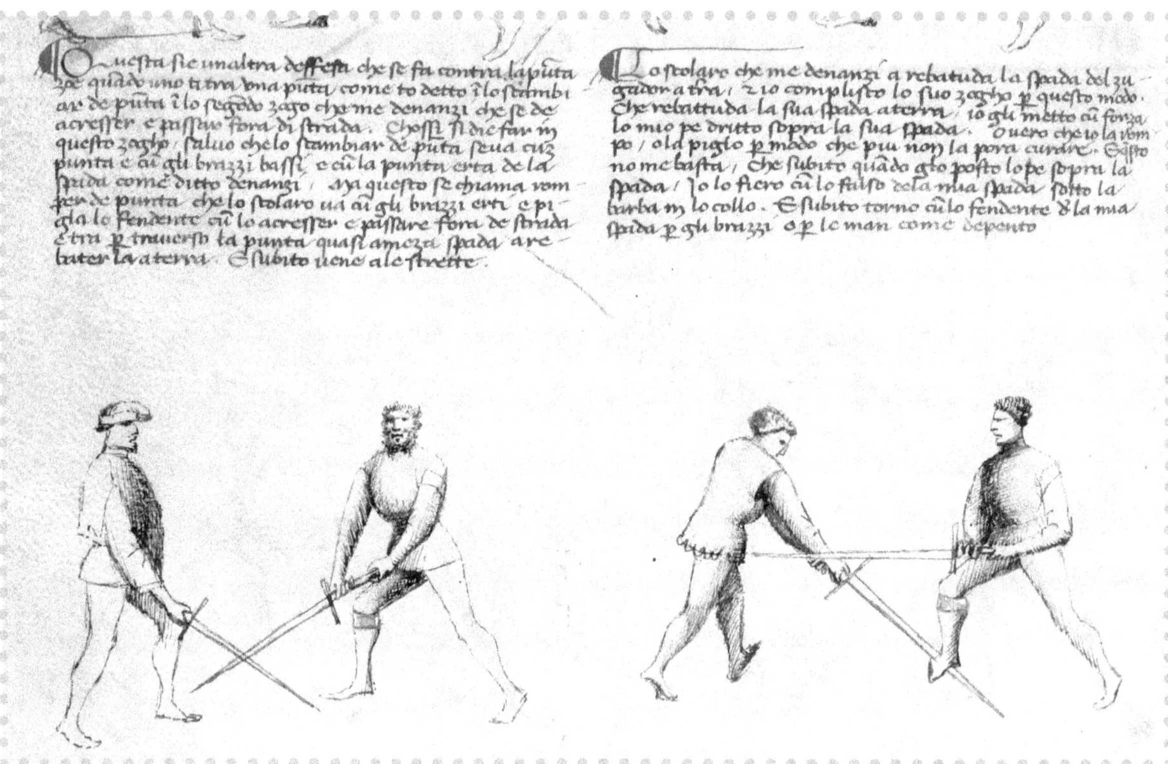

1. You wait in *tutta porta di ferro*. Your partner is in *dente di zenghiaro*.

2. They enter with a thrust to your belly.

3. Beat their sword down, stepping offline and passing across…

4. Keeping your hands low, stroke your false edge across the bib of their mask, and let the sword continue round to strike a *roverso fendente* to their head.

Breaking the thrust
https://guywindsor.net/aw1044

Notes

THE SEVENTH CLASS

This class is about breadth. Let's see how much you already know, expand on it a bit, and give you the diagnostic tools to establish how much you can remember.

If you haven't done the fifth class yet, it would be best to go back and do that now. This class will add the eighth play of the first master, and it would make sense if you've covered plays 3, 4, 5 and 6 first. Warm up as usual, touch base with your falling practice and the four guards drill, then:

First master, eighth play

The eighth play of the first master is a variation on the initial cover.

1. Attacker and defender both in *porta di ferro*, left foot forwards.

2. Attacker passes to strike with a *fendente*, aiming at the mask.

3. Intercept the attacker's wrist with your left hand while stepping to your left, catching the outside of their wrist or the back of their hand.

4. Using the momentum of their strike, redirect the dagger into their thigh or belly.

First master of dagger, eighth play
https://guywindsor.net/aw1045

Notes

The first eight plays of the first master, as a unit

The first eight plays of the first master are presented on a two-page spread of the manuscript, and take this form:

- Cover and disarm; counter to the disarm.

- Cover and lock; counter to the lock.

- Cover and break; counter to the break.

- Cover and takedown.

- Alternative to the cover.

This is a beautiful little zip file of the whole dagger section, if you think about it. It includes all 'five things' (strike, disarm, lock, break, takedown), counters to them, and a reference to the idea that there is more than one way to counter. The takedown has no counter at the point it is shown in the manuscript, because once the play has got that far, it's over. But you can certainly prevent the takedown with the second play (the counter to the disarm). So now that you know all eight plays, practise them in order to see how readily each one comes to mind. It's worth learning this block of material by rote because when you run through it, you will find areas of weakness and areas of strength. Which plays are you best at? Which do you find hard to remember? Which can you do choreographically, but not against much actual pressure?

First eight plays of the dagger
https://guywindsor.net/aw1046

Notes

Run a diagnostic

Now that you have the first eight plays as a unit, run through them quite quickly, to find the weakest link. Is your counter to the lock working? Can you do the alternative cover? Do you actually know the sequence well enough that you don't have to think about the choreography? There is always something to work on.

So, having run the diagnostic, and found the weakest link, see if you can improve it. Use what you already know about how to train to work on the problem at the optimal rate of failure. At this stage, we are just working on technical skill, not tactical choices, so you don't need to worry about choosing the right technique yet.

Once the thing you are working on seems to be better, run the diagnostic again. Here are the possible outcomes:

1. The thing we worked on is no longer the weakest link. In that case, find the next weakest link and work on that.

2. The thing we worked on is still the weakest link, but it's better than it was. So keep working at it, using the same approach as before.

3. The thing we worked on is still the weakest link, and doesn't seem to have improved. Find another way to work on it.

When training you are always either learning something new or getting better at something you already know. If you are ever not sure what to work on, run a diagnostic; fix the weakest link; run the diagnostic again.

At the moment, we are looking primarily at breadth. How much of what we have covered can you remember?

Notes

Longsword diagnostics

Take up the sword and run through some handling drills, the blows that you know, part one of the cutting drill perhaps, and then review all four of the basic drills: first, second, break, exchange.

Now you know the basic process of running a diagnostic, and have reviewed your current knowledge base, let's find your weakest link.

What are the diagnostic drills for longsword?

Any drill can be used diagnostically. For example, if you are working through first drill, you can run it as a diagnostic to check whether you remember the whole drill, and if so, which step is the weakest?

* Is the attack done in good form, to the right target, without losing concentration as you recover out of measure?

* Is the parry–riposte done correctly, with the right footwork, and can you do it under a bit of pressure?

* Are you transitioning smoothly from the *mandritto fendente* to the cover and pommel strike, and are you actually covered against the riposte?

* Is your counter to the pommel strike effortless and mechanically sound?

* Which is the weakest of the four steps, for you and for your partner?

Having found what you could be working on, you then have to figure out how to improve it. Firstly, do you know the choreography? If not, learn that. Once that's down, can you perform the action at the right time, in the right place, with the appropriate amount of force, against a reasonable attempt by your partner to stop you?

Start by running through all four of the basic drills, and seeing which one is the weakest for you. First drill, second drill, the break, or the exchange? Then go back to the instructions if necessary, and work on bringing that drill up to the standard of the others.

Then go through that drill, and find the weakest step, and, you guessed it, bring it up to the standard of the others.

Notes

PREPARATION FOR THE EIGHTH CLASS

You will need a new training tool for the last class in this workbook: a pell. Depending on what's available to you, and how handy you are, this may take some time to acquire.

The pell is a post, often with a crossbeam, fixed upright for you to cut and thrust at. Any old post will do. It doesn't have to be very stable, because you won't hit it hard. When teaching in salles without a pell, we have improvised with a broom propped up between two chairs. The pell can be developed into a sophisticated machine with arms, joints, perhaps a spring-loaded sword built in (really! my students are very inventive). But it doesn't have to be: my own pell in my garden at home is just a fence post with a couple of bits of wood screwed to the bottom to keep it upright.

THE EIGHTH CLASS

In this final class of the beginners' course, we won't add any new plays or techniques. Instead, we will look at how to structure a training session, and using the wall target and the pell to improve your control over the sword.

The usual format for one of my regular *armizare* classes is this:

* opening salute

* warm-up

* footwork exercises and games

* dagger and/or *abrazare* drills related to the topic of the class

* longsword handling and striking drills

* longsword pair drills (which may include freeplay)

* closing salute

* time allowed for students to warm themselves down, and/or do conditioning or free training.

The warm-up functions to get people out of their everyday life and into their bodies, as well as preparing the body for various kinds of exercise. The footwork exercises and games get people moving in the way the system requires. Dagger and *abrazare* drills let us work on fundamentals like timing, measure, tactical training and so on, at a higher, more intense level, without having to worry about weapon control. Then the longsword section of the class starts with getting control of the weapon, before working with partners who are depending on that control for their safety.

The salutes provide a clear beginning and end to the class.

This structure is not written in stone. We may drop the longsword stuff and focus on dagger, or spear, or some other part of the system.

In any one session, you should have one clear thing you are working on. Footwork precision, for example. Whatever else you are doing, you are paying attention to the footwork. Or perhaps timing. Or choreography of longer drills. It doesn't matter, so long as you choose something sensible, then work on it.

For now, please plan and run a session, from warm-up to longsword handling. When you've got some handling drills done, move on to the next bit of this chapter.

Notes

The problem with training with partners is that you must keep them safe. This means you can't train at the level at which you are struggling to retain control of the sword. You need a safety margin.

That is where inanimate targets come in. The pell, for instance. There are no moral consequences for going a bit too fast and hard and really bashing the pell. This means you can push the envelope a bit, without risking your partner's health.

So, set up the pell, and:

Exercises on the pell

- Starting out of measure, get into measure and do the striking sequence that is step one of first drill.

- Then do the same with step one of second drill.

- Pick one blow, and see how hard and fast you can strike at the pell without touching it.

- Repeat with multiple strikes (use your imagination!). Strike fast, but stroke the pell gently on a marked spot (about as hard as you would like to be hit in freeplay). See how hard and fast that really is.

- Repeat with multiple strikes in different lines.

- Choose a specific strike, and approach the pell from far away, moving smoothly and without stopping with blows from guard to guard: see if you can arrive in measure with your sword in the right place to launch the prearranged strike. This is harder than it sounds.

- The 99 strikes exercise: make 100 cuts at the pell, without touching it. Every time you touch it, the counter resets to zero. So if you touch on strike 99, you go back to the beginning…

Once you have spent some time on the pell, move one to one or other of the basic drills, and notice how much slower you move when you're being careful of your partner's safety. Solo training on the pell can be liberating!

Using the Pell
https://guywindsor.net/aw1047

WHAT NEXT?

Well done getting through the beginners' course. We have laid the foundation for your progress in the art of arms, and you will be relying on the things you have learned in this book for the rest of your *armizare* career. But it doesn't have to stop here…

The Armizare Workbook Two

Now that you have completed the beginners' course, it's time to add depth and breadth. Volume two of this series contains the following eight classes:

* Ninth Class: this adds plays of the fourth master of dagger, includes lots of revision, and then explodes your options with the four corners drill.

* Tenth Class: this explores the rear-weighted guards.

* Eleventh Class: this adds feints, including the *punta falsa*, to your repertoire.

* Twelfth Class: this class completes the cutting drill, putting everything you have learned so far into a memorable drill you can practice.

The last four classes are not intended to be taken in order – choose which you would like next:

* How to Train: this class teaches you how to develop your skills, whatever aspect of the art you focus on.

* Mechanics of Striking: this class examines the details of generating power and keeping control of the weapon. We have covered some of this in the last class of this book.

* The Dagger: this class covers all nine masters of the dagger, and the five things (disarm, strike, lock, break and takedown), such that you can do all five things with all nine masters.

* *Largo* and *Stretto*: this class covers the details of wide and constrained play: what that really means, and how you can apply it in tactical decision making.

Once you have worked through these 16 lessons, you will have a thorough grounding in the practice of *armizare*. But there's much more ground to cover: there are the 20 plays of *abrazare* to work through (you know six), the 76 plays of the dagger (you know about half), the plays of the sword in one hand (you know the first couple), the 20 plays of the *zogho largo* (you know most of them), the 23 plays of the *zogho stretto* (you know about half of them), and then there's armoured combat on foot with the sword, axe, and spear, and all the mounted combat too!

But Fiore's art is presented in *Il Fior di Battaglia* as a system. With the basics you already have, you can reasonably approach any other part of the manuscript (though you would need to be a very good rider to start on the mounted combat plays).

Other books and courses

The resources I can provide to help you, in addition to volume two, include:

For the dagger: my book *The Medieval Dagger*, and my online course *The Medieval Dagger Course*.

For the longsword: my books *The Medieval Longsword*, *Advanced Longsword: Form and Function*, and *From Medieval Manuscript to Modern Practice*. And my online course *The Complete Longsword Course*.

I have yet to write a book on the spear, pollax, armoured combat, or mounted combat (though I have a collaboration in the works that might address the latter).

The best value package I have at the moment is the *Mastering the Art of Arms* subscription, which gives you access to all the courses, and ebook copies of all the books, for a modest monthly fee.

GLOSSARY

The table below includes words that are either unique to fencing sources, or have a specific technical meaning in a fencing context. There are still some areas of debate amongst scholars of these arts; where I am aware of such, I have mentioned so in the comments. The translations are not necessarily applicable to modern Italian or other historical sources. Students should also note that the terms are often spelled several different ways in the original sources.

Italian grammar is quite simple, but has some aspects that English speakers may find odd – not least that a single word may have different forms, and to make a word plural, we can't just throw an 's' on the end. In general, nouns are either masculine or feminine, and adjectives will have both masculine and feminine forms that agree with the noun they describe. For example: *punta falsa*, false thrust. *Filo falso*, false edge.

In general:

* Nouns ending in -e when singular will end in -i when plural: *fendente, fendenti*.

* Nouns ending in -o when singular will end in -i when plural: *colpo, colpi*.

* Nouns ending in -a when singular will end in -e when plural: *ligadura, ligadure*.

While it is standard practice to place all adjectives in their masculine form first, in the list below I have placed each word in the form that is most commonly used in Fiore (e.g. *longa*), and I have used the spellings that you will find in Fiore and/or Vadi's manuscripts, such as *zogho*, which would be *gioco* in modern Italian.

These terms are frequently combined: for example, *mandritto fendente* is a forehand descending blow.

Italian	English	Comments
Abrazare	To wrestle	
Accrescere	To step forwards	Without passing.
Bicorno	Two-horned	A guard.
Breve, posta breve	Short; short guard	Refers to a specific guard position.
Cinghiare/cinghiaro	Wild boar	The name of a specific guard position.
Colpo/i	A blow or strike	
Corona	Crown	The name of a specific guard position.

Italian	English	Comments
Coverta	Cover, parry	
Destro/a	On the right	
Discrescere	To step back	Without passing.
Donna	Woman	The name of a specific guard position.
Dritto, diritto, derito	Right, forehand or true	*Filo* or *taglio dritto* is the true edge.
Elzo	Hilt; crossguard	
Falcon	Falcon	The name of a specific guard position.
Falso	False edge, back edge	
Fendente	Descending blow	Usually qualified by *mandritto / dritto* (forehand) or *roverso* (backhand).
Finestra	Window	The name of a specific guard position.
Fora/for di strada	Out of the way	Usually used in connection with a footwork action: thus *passo fora di strada*, 'pass out of the way'.
Frontale	Frontal, a guard	
Giocco/giocho stretto	Close, narrow or constrained play	
Giocho largho	Wide play	
Gioco, giocho	Play	This is used to describe a single sequence (such as the first play of the sword) and, when qualified as *largo* or *stretto*, the tactical situation.
Incrosare/incroce	Crossing. Also parry	
Largo	Wide	Used in contrast to *stretto*. A state of play, or tactical situation, in which you are free to strike.
Lunga/longa	Long	Part of the name of a specific guard position, *posta lunga con la spada curta*.
Mandritto	Forehand	See *dritto/diritto*.
Mantener	Handle of the sword	
Meza spada/mezza spada	Half sword	A crossing made near the middle of both blades.
Mezana porta di ferro	Middle iron door	A guard position.

Italian	English	Comments
Mezano/i	Middle blows, horizontal blows	
Passare	To pass, as in stepping	
Passo	A pass, also the length of a passing step, also the space between your feet when standing	
Porta di ferro	Iron door.	Can also be 'middle' (*mezana*) or 'flat ground' (*piana terena*).
Posta/poste	Position or guard	Used more commonly than *guardia*.
Quatro dita	'Four fingers'	A unit of measurement.
Rebattere	To beat aside – to parry	
Remedio	Remedy; the defence against an attack	
Rendopiare/reddopiare	Redouble	To strike again. Note: in 16th century Bolognese sources, *ridoppio* is a rising blow with the true edge, from the left. This is not the case here.
Riverso/roverso	Backhand	
Rompere	To break, as in the breaking of the thrust	
Rota	'Turn' from *rotare*. A rising blow	Used by Vadi only. This blow gets its own chapter, chapter XV. It is also used on 15r in *rota da molin*, 'millwheel'.
Sagitaria	Archer	Refers to specific guard positions, used differently by Fiore and Vadi.
Scambiare	To exchange, as in to exchange the thrust	
Sinestro	On the left	
Somesso	The width of a fist	A unit of measurement.
Sottano	A rising blow	
Stancho	Left (side or foot, usually)	In modern Italian, 'tired'.
Strada	Way	This is used in the sense of the direct line between the two combatants. Hence to step *fora di strada*, 'out of the way', is to step off the line.

Italian	English	Comments
Stramazone	A whirling blow from the wrist	
Stretto/stretta/strette	Close, constrained, narrow.	
Taglio/e	Cut, but also cutting edge	
Traverso; ala traversa	Across, or diagonal	Usually used in connection with a footwork action: *va for de strada per traverso passo*; 'go out of the way with a pass across.'
Tondo	'Round': a horizontal blow	
Tornare	'To return'; to pass back	
Vera croce	True cross	A guard position (sword in armour).
Volta	Turn	Specifically *volta stabile* (stable turn: when with both feet fixed you can play on the same side in front and behind), *meza volta* (half turn: when with a pass forwards or backwards you can play on the other side), *tutta volta* (whole turn: when one foot remains fixed and the other turns around it).
Vista, visteggiare	Feint, to feint	This use of the word is absolutely clear from its context.
Volante/volanti	'Flying,' a horizontal blow	This term is unique to Vadi.
Zenghiaro	Wild boar	A guard.
Zogho largo	Wide play	See giocco largo.
Zogho stretto	Close play	See giocco stretto.

FURTHER READING

If you are practising the Art of Arms, you may find my online courses helpful. You can find the courses and get 50% off your first month with this link: guywindsor.net/solo50

Prefer to read? You might like some of these.

On Training in General
The Windsor Method: the Principles of Solo Training: the self-help book for people who want to add years to their life and life to their years. In this refreshingly straight-forward and gentle guide I lay out the fundamental principles behind personal development and excellence in any field. How? By establishing a solid foundation, and a step-by-step approach to mechanics and training. This is The Windsor Method: use it to guide your practice and elevate your skills.

On Fiore's Art of Arms:
Mastering the Art of Arms, Book 1: The Medieval Dagger A training manual for Fiore's dagger material, by Guy Windsor. This is a complete overview of the dagger material in Fiore's art of arms, and includes instruction on how to fall, how to develop real skills, as well as covering all of the fundamental attacks with and defences against the dagger. Hardback available from Spada Press, paperback and ebook from Freelance Academy Press.

Mastering the Art of Arms, Book 2: The Medieval Longsword. A training manual for Fiore's longsword material. If you want to learn how to train and fight with a longsword in an authentic medieval style, this book is for you. This book features an introduction by the excellent historical novelist and medieval combatant, Christian Cameron.

Mastering the Art of Arms, Book 3: Advanced Longsword, Form and Function This covers using forms for skill development, and a lot of Fiore-specific training, building on the groundwork laid in *The Medieval Longsword*.

From Medieval Manuscript to Modern Practice: the Longsword Techniques of Fiore dei Liberi. This has my transcription, translation, commentary, and links to video clips of my interpretation of all of Fiore's longsword plays on foot out of armour, as well as a thorough introduction.

The Swordsman's Companion. A training manual for medieval longsword. This was my first book, and it has become something of a classic in this field. As a training manual, it is largely replaced by *The Medieval Longsword*, but as a book about how and why to train, it is still relevant.

The Armizare Vade Mecum. Mnemonic verses for remembering Fiore's art. This is a collection of verses, each one of which encapsulates one element of Fiore's art.

On Vadi's Art of Arms:

The Art of Sword Fighting in Earnest. An accurate translation of Filippo Vadi's *De Arte Gladiatoria Dimicandi*, with a detailed introduction, commentary from a practical swordsmanship perspective, and a full glossary. This book was examined as part of my PhD, so it's been academically vetted at the highest level.

On Historical Martial Arts:

The Theory and Practice of Historical Martial Arts. This book includes all seven instalments of *The Swordsman's Quick Guide,* as well as extensive instruction on recreating historical martial arts from historical sources, how to train, how to teach, even how to get better sleep.

Swordfighting, for Writers, Game Designers, and Martial Artists. This book is made up of about 50% posts from my blog and 50% new material, and does exactly what it says in the title. It also features an introduction from the one and only Neal Stephenson, author of *Snow Crash, The Diamond Age,* and *The Baroque Cycle,* to name but a few.

On Capoferro's Rapier method:

The Duellist's Companion. A training manual for 17th century Italian rapier. This is still the standard work on the interpretation and practice of Capoferro's rapier system.

The Rapier Workbooks:

These workbooks comprise a complete training method for becoming proficient at Capoferro's style of rapier fencing. Each workbook is designed to lie flat, with abundant space for note-taking, and with a linked video clip for every action. They are available laid out for right or left handers, to make note-taking easier.

The Rapier Workbook Part 1, Beginners
The Rapier Workbook Part 2, Completing the Basics
The Rapier Workbook Part 3, Developing Your Skills
The Rapier Workbook Part 4, Sword and Dagger and Sword and Cape

ABOUT THE AUTHOR

Dr. Guy Windsor is a bestselling author, teacher, lecturer, and one of the top experts on historical swordfighting and martial systems in the world. A graduate of the prestigious Edinburgh University, where he received a PhD for his seminal work analyzing and recreating historical martial arts, Dr. Windsor has written numerous bestselling (and acclaimed) books in his areas of expertise. He also founded The School of European Swordsmanship in Helsinki, Finland, and has taught students, martial artists, and media professionals all over the world how to fight, train, and entertain. Find him at his website, GuyWindsor.net.

THANKS

Thanks are due first to Zachariah Chamberlaine, Curtis Fee, and Dave Smith, for being my demonstration partners in the video clips. The clips are mostly taken from my Medieval Dagger, and Medieval Longsword courses, though some were shot especially for this book.

Thanks also to my assistants Kate Tilton and Katie Mackenzie, who between them make sure all the ayes are drotted and teas crussed in the back end of the publishing process. They can also take a joke.

Nick Venables created the covers, exceeding my expectations as usual (he also did a superb job on the re-branding of *The Medieval Dagger*, *The Medieval Longsword*, and *Advanced Longsword: Form and Function*).

Bek Pickard of Zebedee Design has done another lovely job of laying out this rather demanding format. She's worked on most of my books since 2012, and I don't know what I'd do without her.

And to my editor Andrew Chapman who very helpfully found 944 things to fix in this book. Literally. 944. I *thought* it was pretty clean when I sent it.

And to my students, especially those who bought the Rapier Workbooks in which I pioneered this workbook format. Their positive response to this way of presenting my Art has been very encouraging.